KW-450-637

For my wife, Asami, whose tireless work for our
family allows me to indulge in these silly adventures.

DESTINATION
FLAVOUR
PEOPLE AND PLACES

ADAM LIAW

Hardie Grant
BOOKS

SBS

CONTENTS

INTRODUCTION

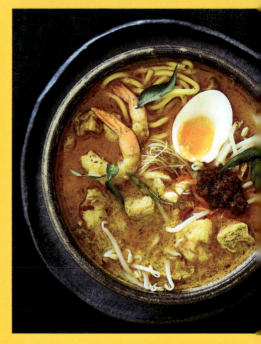

Page 1: Lion's head meatballs in Shanghai, China
Pages 2–3: Herding reindeer with Sami herders, Målselv, Norway
Pages 4–5: XunPu Village, Fujian, China
Top: Sunset over Chirihama Beach, Ishikawa, Japan
Bottom left: Oysters in Freycinet, Tasmania, Australia
Bottom right: Chicken & prawn laksa (page 234)

I might actually have the best job in the world.

When I was young, travelling the world and eating great food was certainly my dream, but I think the part that my childhood daydreams missed was why it is that food and travel seem to so often go hand in hand.

There is little we look forward to on the road more than a good meal, but eating while travelling is about more than just the hunt for your next feed. We travel for the insight it gives us into another way of life, another side of our own humanity. Whether a place on earth might be separated from our own by distance or time, or both, the chance to experience that place gives us a perspective on the people who live there, and also the chance to see ourselves reflected in them.

EVERY SINGLE DISH AROUND THE WORLD HAS AN INCREDIBLE STORY TO TELL.

Take a laksa (page 234), for example. The universally loved bowl of soup and noodles can be enjoyed just as a meal, but every ingredient in it is a breadcrumb along a trail far richer than the soup itself. Follow the clues and you will reveal its history.

Laksa originated hundreds of years ago across Thailand, Malaysia, Indonesia and what is now modern Singapore, but its origins go back even further to the Chinese province of Fujian, located in China's south below the Yangtze, where rice is the preferred grain compared to the wheat and millet more popular in the drier climate to the north. Fujian's geography combines rich agricultural lands and mountains with an abundance of seafood from along the coast. The cuisine often combines food from the land and sea together, and is known for its love of soups and broths.

In Fujian you'll also find cities like Xiamen and Quanzhou, which operated as trading ports along the Maritime Silk Route, connecting China with the world through Southeast Asia, the Indian Subcontinent, the Arabian Peninsula, Africa and Europe. Often Fujian's famous seafoods were dried for trade over the long nautical journeys.

In the local dialect Fujian is known as Hokkien, and some Hokkien sailors who travelled the route settled in Southeast Asia. Over centuries dozens of new fusion cultures of Straits Chinese developed throughout the region – the Eurasian Kristang, Indo–Chinese Chittys, the Baba-Yayas in Thailand, Arab–Indo–Chinese Jawi-Pekan in Penang and the Peranakans of Melaka and Singapore.

The Peranakan combined Chinese culture with that of their newfound homes abroad, and their new communities grew through the prosperity of trade.

But what does this have to do with laksa, you might ask? Well, everything.

'Laksa' in the Hokkien dialect translates as 'spicy sand'. The 'spice' references the hot dried chillies used in the soup, which were originally traded into Southeast Asia from the Arabian Peninsula along the very trade routes that brought the Hokkien there. The 'sand' is a reference to the texture of ground dried shrimps, preserved from the waters around Fujian and sent south on the same ships. The belacan (shrimp paste) and aromatic rempah of lemongrass, galangal and other aromatics borrow technique from the Indonesian and Malay schools of cooking that became incorporated by marriage into Peranakan culture.

Even something as simple as the combination of prawns and chicken in its soup, as well as the use of noodles of both rice and wheat, are a direct influence of Fujian cuisine (particularly from Xiamen, where thin rice noodles are especially popular).

You can even see the parallels between laksa and Fujian's popular sachamian ('sand tea noodles'), a laksa-like noodle soup with a base of dried chilli and peanuts that may well have informed both laksa as well as the peanut sauces that are served with satays from Thailand to Malaysia.

Even as you follow laksa across the different Straits Chinese communities you see differences, from the creamy coconut Thai- and Melaka-style laksas to the sour fish and pineapple laksa from Penang.

When you look at laksa through the lens of the people who made it, and still make it today, it becomes so much more than a meal.

It's the story of grand voyages. Of people who left their homes and pointed their boats out into an unfamiliar sea, setting sail for places they'd never been before in search of their fortunes. Of how they fell in love and built empires. A magnificent opera spanning centuries of tragedy and triumph among nameless players, performed silently in a simple bowl of noodles.

ALL FOOD IS THE STORY OF PEOPLE. THE FOOD WE EAT REFLECTS WHERE WE LIVE, WHERE WE CAME FROM, THE CROPS WE CHOOSE TO GROW, THE FISH WE CHOOSE TO CATCH, WHO WE SHARE OUR MEALS WITH AND HOW WE SPEND OUR DAYS. THREE TIMES A DAY, ALL OVER THE WORLD, OUR MEALS KEEP THE RHYTHM OF EVERYDAY LIFE.

The chance to travel the world exploring this connection between food, culture and people has been a privilege I will never take for granted.

It might appear on-screen like one big, fun adventure (and at times it certainly is), but the magic of television is to make difficult things look very easy. We don't show the hard work that goes into every series. We spend months researching: dozens of people with their heads in books, online, on the phone and even flying to remote parts of the world to chase down a lead.

On the road we live at a frantic pace, rarely spending more than a night or two in the same place. There's barely enough time to chat to the families we miss back home and maybe get a little laundry done before it's on to the next town to meet someone new with a great story to tell. It's a rinse-and-repeat process that goes on for months (each series takes about three months of travel to film) and by the end we're exhausted, physically and mentally.

But even after we've come home there's no rest. More months of post-production follow with editing, script writing, sound mixing, titles, graphics and fact-checking. That the final result is played out on television in just half an hour makes me feel a mix of relief, sadness and pride. Relief because we have finished, sadness because months of work whiz by in just a few minutes on-screen, and pride because honestly I think our whole team does an amazing job realising what we try to achieve.

I'm certainly not complaining about the hard work, but I wanted to tell you what it takes for us to put this show together to illustrate that we don't do it just for the fun of it. Of course it's fun at times, but I also feel we're doing something very worthwhile. The chance to peek even briefly into the life, or onto the dinner plate, of someone on the other side of the world from the comfort of your sofa is not something that happens easily. To make sure that tiny glimpse is presented respectfully, accurately, in the appropriate context and with genuine heart and emotion is a responsibility that we take very seriously.

I know to many who have seen *Destination Flavour* it's just a bit of light entertainment, but to us it's a chance to show you the everyday lives of people you would otherwise never get to meet. It's a food program, but it's not a program about food. In the same way that music uses notes to tell stories larger than their frequencies, we use food to tell stories about people.

Kiritanpo nabe, Akita, Japan

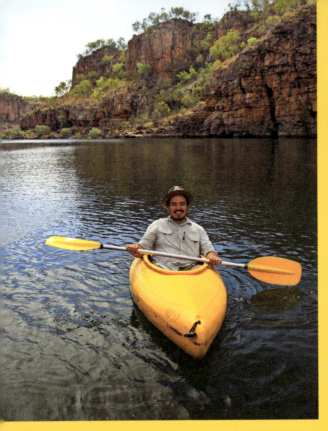

Top left: Kayaking the Nitmiluk Gorges, Northern Territory, Australia

Top middle: *Rushan*, fried cow's milk, scattered with sugar; a Bai minority delicacy in Yunnan, China

Top right: Otomezushi, Kanazawa, Japan

Bottom left: Wakasagi ice fishing on Lake Akan, Hokkaido, Japan

Bottom right: A 'Michael Jackson' at a hawker centre in Singapore

Writing this book has been a chance to revisit the memories of my travels, and in that process of recollection it is the people I have met that come to mind more than any meal that I ate.

> **THIS BOOK IS FULL OF RECIPES THAT TELL THE STORIES OF THE PEOPLE WE MET, AS WELL AS NEW RECIPES THAT COMPLETE THE STORIES WE WEREN'T ABLE TO TELL ON-SCREEN.**

In the northern reaches of Scandinavia I dogsledded out into the white wilderness of the Arctic and herded reindeer with Johan and Karen Anders, reindeer-herding Sami who taught me their culture through a simple dish of stewed reindeer and sweet pancakes made from reindeer blood. The details of that memory are on page 117.

In New Zealand, a man named Hans Biemond has fed his family for decades with wild game hunted from the hills around his property. I made a pie (page 210) from the hare, boar and deer meat he gave me, and ate it looking over Lake Wakatipu and its snow-dusted mountains.

In Singapore I met a long-lost cousin who had spent half a lifetime running a hawker stall serving just one dish. The lessons Liow Tong Thong taught me are incorporated, along with the lessons taught me by my mother and grandmother, into my recipe for Hainanese chicken rice on page 222. It's a dish closer to my heart than any other.

In Japan my mother-in-law, Miki Fujitsuka, showed me how to make Nikujaga (page 161), and now when I make it for my wife and children in Australia it tastes just like a memory from her childhood.

In Australia's Northern Territory, in a town called Humpty Doo, a gentle giant named Steve Sunk (page 45) made me a set of knives in his back shed, and showed me how to fillet a crocodile. I used that crocodile to make a laksa, a favourite dish in the Territory, and another unlikely chapter in laksa's extraordinary story.

Yes, this is a book about food and travel, but more than that it is a book about people.

I hope you like their stories.

AUSTRALIA

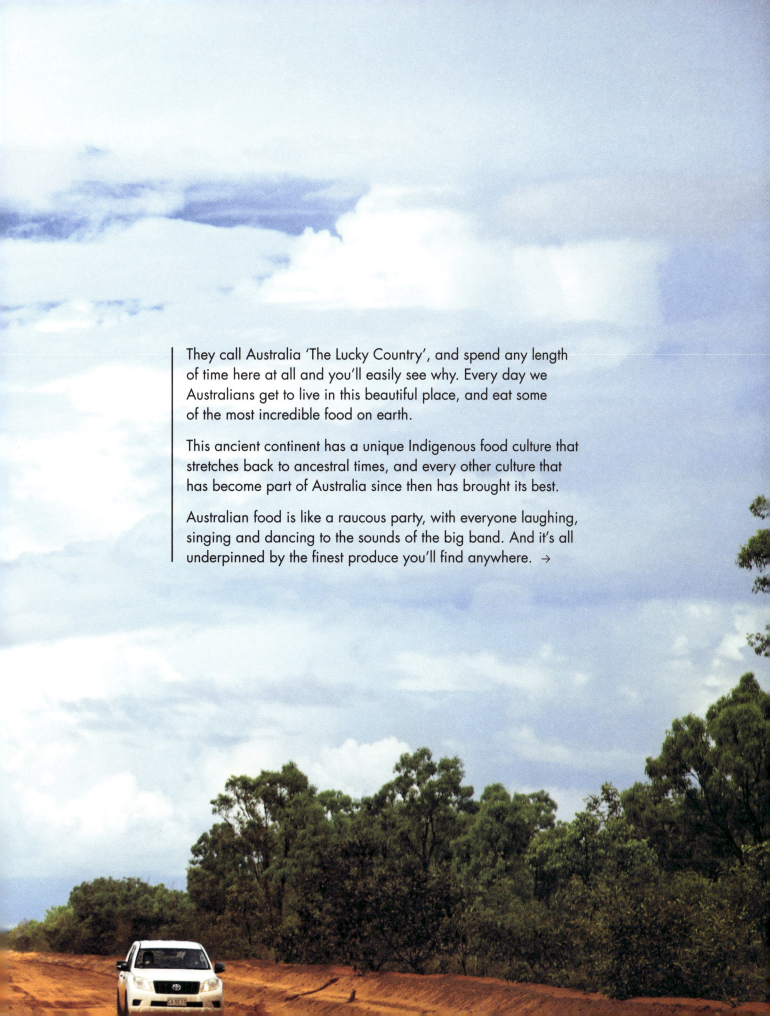

They call Australia 'The Lucky Country', and spend any length of time here at all and you'll easily see why. Every day we Australians get to live in this beautiful place, and eat some of the most incredible food on earth.

This ancient continent has a unique Indigenous food culture that stretches back to ancestral times, and every other culture that has become part of Australia since then has brought its best.

Australian food is like a raucous party, with everyone laughing, singing and dancing to the sounds of the big band. And it's all underpinned by the finest produce you'll find anywhere. →

Australia's world-class produce isn't a lucky accident of geography. Produce is as much about people as it is about soil, air and water. A good fish in the sea is one thing, but a good fish on the dinner table takes a skilled fisherman to catch it, to treat it with care, and to get it to your dinner table in its best condition. Give two farmers identical plots of land and what comes out of it will be more a testament to their talent and dedication than the natural conditions of the earth.

Australians often look outward for inspiration, gazing longingly at the rich food cultures of Europe and Asia, as if our own is somehow less worthy than lauded cuisines like those of France, Italy and Japan.

But in Australia we often don't realise how good we have it. We look at a dish like Mud crab in mango and tamarind sambal (page 22) and think it's from Asia, yet the ingredients and cooking techniques involved came to northwestern Australia centuries ago.

A dish like that has a longer Australian history than Vegemite.

Fish and chips? England may claim it, but if the first fish-and-chip shop was set up in London in 1860, and in Australia in 1879 by Athanasias Comino on Sydney's Oxford Street, I'll be damned if 150 years later we're still thinking of fish and chips as English food. Plus, the Brits have never had theirs with King George whiting (page 33).

Even when it comes to pavlova (page 60), debate rages between Australia and New Zealand over who made it first (and let me put that to rest: the Kiwis did) – but frankly, who cares? It's Australia's best-loved dessert and, with due thanks and credit to the baker in New Zealand who whipped it up more than a century ago, it's ours now too, and Christmas wouldn't be the same without it.

Dishes enter cuisines from all over. Tempura (page 151) came to Japan from Portugal – but you don't see the Japanese calling it Portuguese food.

Australian cuisine may have arrived here from every corner, but it has been welcomed with open arms. In every little town in the whole country there'll be a pub and a Chinese restaurant, and both of them will be serving Australian food – one with English origins and the other with Chinese.

In the broad church of Australian food you can't tell me that a dish like salt and pepper squid, which is found all around the country but hardly anywhere abroad, is any less Australian than a meat pie. Australian food tells the whole story of Australia, but sometimes we don't even realise how Australian it really is.

Pages 12–3: Cape Leveque Road, Western Australia
Top: Cape Leveque, Western Australia
Bottom left: Jauma barrel room, Basket Range, South Australia
Bottom middle: Happy pigs in the Victorian High Country
Bottom right: Moreton Island, Queensland

The slight bitterness of gin is a wonderful complement to the metallic tang of oysters. Gin and tonic lovers should get around this one.

OYSTERS WITH GIN & DILL VINAIGRETTE

PREPARATION 5 MINUTES +
10 MINUTES CHILLING
FOR 2 DOZEN OYSTERS

24 large Pacific oysters,
   scrubbed clean and
   shucked, on the half shell
lemon wedges, to serve

GIN & DILL VINAIGRETTE
1 tablespoon chopped dill
1 tablespoon grated
   eschalot
1 tablespoon grated
   cucumber, seeds and
   skin removed
50 ml extra-virgin olive oil
50 ml rice vinegar or
   apple-cider vinegar
1 tablespoon lemon juice
1 tablespoon gin
a pinch of sugar

Combine all the vinaigrette ingredients in a screw-top jar and shake to combine. Chill in the fridge for 10 minutes, then shake again.

Spoon a little of the vinaigrette over each oyster and serve with the lemon wedges.

NOTE Oysters on ice look great, but when the ice melts it can leave you with a big puddle of trouble. I prefer to serve them on a 'wet' salt – mix rock salt and cooking salt together with just enough water to shape it into a mouldable pile, then chill it in the fridge. It will keep the oysters cold and upright, and won't melt into a clean-up job later.

Since I made these for our *Destination Flavour* Christmas Special many years ago, they've become a bit of a staple for any special family gathering. Choose soft, sweet buns, and make sure you give them lots of love with the tomalley butter.

LOBSTER ROLLS

PREPARATION 15 MINUTES +
30 MINUTES CHILLING
COOKING 15 MINUTES
SERVES 8

1 live lobster, weighing about 1.5 kg

¾ cup (185 ml) Japanese mayonnaise

1 eschalot, finely chopped

1 celery stalk, finely chopped

1 tablespoon finely chopped chives

1 tablespoon finely shredded parsley

2 tablespoons lemon juice

50 g butter

8 dinner rolls or small hot dog buns, halved

8 cornichons

SHELLFISH BOIL

2 bay leaves

1 teaspoon fennel seeds

1 teaspoon chilli flakes

1 teaspoon black peppercorns

1 teaspoon coriander seeds

1 tablespoon salt

2 star anise

1 brown onion, halved

2 lemons, halved

½ cup (125 ml) white vinegar

Chill the lobster in the freezer for about 30 minutes to put it to sleep. Add the ingredients for the shellfish boil to a large pot big enough to hold the lobster, and add about 8 cups (2 litres) water. Bring the water to a simmer and simmer for 10 minutes. Add the lobster and poach slowly for 15 minutes, then transfer to a bowl of ice to chill for about 10 minutes.

Remove the meat from the tail and legs of the lobster, and remove and reserve the tomalley from the head. (The tomalley is the digestive gland of the lobster found in the head, appearing as a green to yellow-orange mass.)

Cut the lobster meat into 2 cm pieces and combine in a bowl with the mayonnaise, eschalot, celery, chives, parsley and lemon juice. Mix well and season with salt and freshly ground black pepper.

In a small saucepan, combine the tomalley and butter and warm over medium heat, mashing the tomalley with a fork until the butter turns light brown.

Lightly toast the cut sides of the buns and brush liberally with the tomalley butter. Add the lobster mixture and secure the lid of each bun with a cornichon on a skewer.

NOTE If you have a crowd to feed and don't want to drop a small fortune on lobster alone, you can add other seafood as you like. I often make 'Lobster, prawn and crab rolls' for a bigger crowd by adding chopped poached prawns and picked spanner crabmeat to the mix. It's not exactly a budget meal, but the prawns do make a bit of lobster and crab go a long way.

BRIAN LEE

THE FIRST THING YOU NOTICE ABOUT THE DAMPIER PENINSULA, ON THE NORTH-WEST COAST OF WESTERN AUSTRALIA, IS THE COLOURS. ANCIENT ROCKS OF BURNT ORANGE LEAD TO PRISTINE WHITE SAND AND CRYSTAL WATERS OF AQUAMARINE, SET AGAINST A CLOUDLESS BLUE SKY. IT'S ONE OF THE MOST BEAUTIFUL PALETTES ON EARTH.

For all the colour of the land, however, it might be the characters of the Kimberley region's Dampier Peninsula that give it the most colour.

Brian Lee is one of the Indigenous owners of the land here, and spends most of his time teaching others about the traditional ways of the Bardi – the Salt Water People.

He showed me the tree under which his grandmother was born, and we walked on middens so enormous I mistook them for sand dunes. The middens are huge piles of shells left behind by the Bardi of long ago; they are physical memories of meals stretching back thousands of years, and tell of a culture so connected to the land it literally becomes part of it.

Strolling out into the mangroves deserted by the water after the giant king tides roll out, Brian taught me how to hunt for mud crabs – pushing a metal rod into the holes to hear the telltale rasp of steel on shell, and then coaxing the animal into a position where a brave hand can pull it from its hiding place, hopefully without losing a finger to its powerful claws.

A successful fishing trip over, we had to hurry back to our four-wheel drive before the tide rushed back in. It would raise the water level by more than three metres and wash away any trace we were ever there.

I love the way food puts things in context. A mud crab in mango and tamarind sambal might not sound like an Australian dish, but its ingredients and cultural clues are tied to the history of the Dampier Peninsula. Since the sixteenth century, Maccassan sailors visited Australia to trade with Indigenous people, planting mango and tamarind trees along the shore in strategic locations to use as navigational aids.

To make this dish I pulled the crab out of the mud myself, and picked the mango and tamarind from the trees around the mangrove, keeping my eyes peeled for crocodiles. What could be more Australian than that?

MUD CRAB IN MANGO & TAMARIND SAMBAL

PREPARATION 20 MINUTES +
30 MINUTES FREEZING
COOKING 30 MINUTES
SERVES 4

1 live mud crab, weighing
   about 1 kg

1 lime, cut into wedges

3 spring onions, finely
   shredded

½ cup loosely packed
   coriander

MANGO & TAMARIND SAMBAL

¼ cup tamarind pulp

8 eschalots, peeled and
   roughly chopped

5 long red chillies,
   roughly chopped

2 bird's eye chillies,
   roughly chopped

3 garlic cloves, bruised

1 tablespoon belacan
   (shrimp paste)

¼ cup (60 ml) vegetable oil

2 tablespoons chopped
   palm sugar

1 tablespoon fish sauce,
   or more to taste

1 large mango, flesh
   finely chopped

1 tomato, halved, seeds
   removed, diced

To prepare your crab humanely, place it in the freezer or submerge in an ice bath for 30 minutes.

Remove the upper shell of the crab, pick off the gills and discard. Clean the crab under running water and drain. Chop the crab in half with a heavy cleaver. Next, divide each half in half again, leaving two legs on each portion. With the back of the cleaver, gently crack each claw – this makes it easier to extract the meat later on. Set aside.

To make the sambal, soak the tamarind pulp in about ¾ cup (185 ml) of boiling water for 5 minutes. Strain the pulp by pushing it through a fine sieve with the back of a spoon; discard any seeds, then set the tamarind water aside.

Purée the eschalots, chillies, garlic and belacan in a small food processor. Heat a wok over medium heat and add the oil. Cook the shallot mixture for 10 minutes, until very fragrant, stirring frequently. Add the tamarind water and palm sugar, stir to combine, then bring to the boil.

Add the crab pieces and fish sauce, and stir to coat. Reduce the heat to medium. Cover with a lid and cook for 15 minutes, tossing the wok occasionally until the crab is cooked through and the shell is bright red. Add the mango and tomato, toss to combine, then immediately remove from the heat. Taste, and adjust the seasoning if necessary.

Transfer the crab and sambal to a platter. Squeeze the lime wedges over the top, garnish with the spring onion and coriander and serve.

NOTE Balancing the sweetness of the mango and palm sugar against the sourness of tamarind and lime juice and the savouriness of the belacan and fish sauce is all important in this dish. If your mangoes are especially sweet, you may need to reduce the palm sugar, or add more fish sauce to keep the dish savoury.

Uluru,
Northern
Territory

Cooking in beautiful locations can seem like it's all just a bit of fun – and it is, most of the time. When we cooked this dish, however, things were a bit different. A long day filming outdoors and gathering pearl oysters in 40°C conditions under the hot Australian sun meant we were all a bit exhausted when it got around to cooking. We found a great spot, too, but hours of lugging hundreds of kilos of cooking and camera gear up a sheer cliff meant the sun was already setting as we were getting started. Luckily, this is a ten-minute dish.

PEARL MEAT SOM TAM

PREPARATION 10 MINUTES +
10 MINUTES RESTING
SERVES 4 AS A SIDE DISH

200 g pearl meat 'ears'
  (see Note)

juice of 1 lime

a pinch of salt

1 large Lebanese cucumber,
  peeled at intervals, seeds
  removed, then shredded

1 small carrot, peeled
  and shredded

¼ cup (50 g) chopped
  green beans, cut into
  3 cm pieces

10 cherry tomatoes, halved

¼ cup (40 g) roasted
  peanuts, lightly crushed

DRESSING

1 teaspoon palm sugar

1 teaspoon caster sugar

juice of 1 lime

1 tablespoon fish sauce,
  or more to taste

1 garlic clove, peeled
  and bruised

2 bird's eye chillies,
  thinly sliced

Using a sharp knife, halve the pearl meat 'ears' horizontally to create thin slivers, or slice finely. Place the pearl meat in a non-reactive bowl, squeeze over the lime juice, sprinkle with a pinch of salt, and mix to combine. Set aside for 10 minutes.

To make the dressing, place the palm sugar, caster sugar and lime juice in a mortar and pound with a pestle until the sugar has completely dissolved. Taste and adjust the seasoning as required. The sugar and lime juice mixture should have a pleasant balance of sweet and sour. If it is too sweet, add a little more lime juice, and if it is too sour add a little more caster sugar. Gradually stir in the fish sauce to taste. Add the garlic and chilli and gently pound until coarsely ground.

Add the cucumber, carrot, beans and tomatoes to the mortar and very gently bruise the ingredients with the pestle. Add the pearl meat and gently mix until well coated. Stir the peanuts through and serve.

NOTE Pearl meat would have to be one of Australia's most rare and prized ingredients. Tasting a bit like a cross between lobster and abalone, it is a by-product of Australia's pearling industry. You can buy frozen pearl meat from a few specialty suppliers, but as it's only harvested from pearl oysters once a year, in remote areas like Broome, it's very rarely available fresh. Substitute fresh scallops instead.

JAMES ERSKINE

I'VE KNOWN JAMES FOR NEARLY THIRTY YEARS – SINCE WE WERE KIDS BACK IN ADELAIDE – AND I'VE HARDLY EVER SEEN HIM WITHOUT A SMILE ON HIS FACE. YOU COULD DESCRIBE HIM AS A BON VIVANT, BUT YOU'D HAVE TO LEAVE OUT THE CONNOTATION OF FRIVOLITY THAT IMPLIES, AS HE'S MADE A HABIT OF COMBINING HIS LOVE OF CONVIVIALITY WITH A TIRELESS WORK ETHIC.

James is a guy who loves food and wine more than just about anyone I know. I remember when I was about seventeen being invited to his house to eat roast venison from a deer he'd hunted himself. The dress was black tie. The occasion? Well, it was a Thursday.

After a decorated career as a sommelier (he was named *Gourmet Traveller*'s Australian Sommelier of the Year back in 2008), he turned his attentions to making wine. One of the new-wave originals who took over the Basket Range region in the Adelaide Hills, James and his contemporaries started turning South Australian wine on its head, with wild, expressive natural wines at the forefront of the movement.

When I asked if I could film with James for the very first season of *Destination Flavour*, I mentioned I wanted to make a carbonara to match with one of the Jauma wines he had at the time. He was excited by the prospect as he had his own pancetta hanging to cure in his barrel room (made with salt he'd dug out of a cave himself). He organised some cheese made by a friend of his a few hills over, gathered eggs from his chickens, and waded into the lake on his property to pull out handfuls of fresh watercress, just in case I needed it.

He also said he'd make a batch of fresh pasta to be ready when I arrived. I protested and said he'd gone to too much trouble. I'd be fine to cook with a bought pasta, after all.

'Adam,' came his stern reply, 'I'm not going to let you do that'.

This recipe always reminds me of my friend James (see page 29), and is not intended to be traditional. I feel like I need to explain myself here, as it seems any time anyone makes anything that isn't a straight-down-the-line carbonara, you can almost feel the entire Roman diaspora gathering the pitchforks. So for a classic Roman carbonara, just follow this recipe but use guanciale (cured pig's cheek) instead of pancetta, and leave out the garlic and watercress.

ADELAIDE HILLS CARBONARA

PREPARATION 10 MINUTES
COOKING 15 MINUTES
SERVES 4

1 bunch watercress; you'll need about 2 cups (60 g) picked leaves

2 tablespoons olive oil

2 garlic cloves, finely chopped

180 g pancetta, cut into thin slivers

500 g dried spaghetti

2 whole eggs, plus 3 egg yolks

2 cups (180 g) grated pecorino

Pick the small stalks and leaves from the watercress, discarding any thick stalks. Heat a frying pan over medium heat, add the oil and sauté the garlic and pancetta slowly for about 5 minutes, to render the fat from the pancetta and toast the garlic. When the fat has rendered, stir the watercress through to wilt it, then remove from the heat.

While the pancetta is cooking, bring a large pot of water to the boil and add a good amount of salt. Add the spaghetti and boil until just al dente.

In a bowl, beat the eggs and extra yolks well, then whisk the pecorino through and grind in plenty of black pepper.

Reserve about ¼ cup (60 ml) of the pasta water, then drain the pasta and return it to the warm pot. Add the pancetta mixture and all the rendered oil, the egg and cheese mixture and the reserved pasta water.

Stir briskly until the oil, egg, cheese and pasta water have combined and emusified to make a creamy sauce that coats the pasta. Serve immediately.

NOTE The key to a creamy carbonara is emulsifying the oil from the cured meat, the egg yolk and cheese with the small amount of pasta water added. In Italian, this blending and finishing process is called *mantecare*, and it's an absolutely vital technique to know if you want to make great pasta and risotto dishes.

My dad worked in Whyalla, on South Australia's Eyre Peninsula, for most of my childhood, and we travelled there a lot during the years I grew up in Adelaide. *Destination Flavour* has taken me all around the planet, but sometimes it takes a long journey to really make you appreciate what's been in front of you the whole time. The seafood from the Eyre Peninsula might be the best in the world, and King George whiting is one of the region's finest fish. It makes a perfect South Australian fish and chips.

I think a lovely undressed salad of interesting ingredients, with just a little lemon juice squeezed over the top, is the perfect match for good fish and chips – a lovely respite from mouthfuls of fried fish and fried potatoes.

KING GEORGE WHITING & CHIPS

PREPARATION 45 MINUTES
COOKING 45 MINUTES
SERVES 4

800 g large starchy potatoes, peeled and cut into thick chips, then soaked in cold water for at least 10 minutes

1 teaspoon salt

2 teaspoons white vinegar

1½ cups (225 g) self-raising flour

375 ml bottle of pale ale, such as Coopers, chilled

8 cups (2 litres) canola oil or other vegetable oil, for deep-frying

800 g King George whiting fillets

sea salt, for seasoning

tartare sauce, to serve

lemon wedges, to serve

CRUDITÉ SALAD

raw vegetables such as lettuce leaves, shredded red cabbage, thinly sliced red onion, cherry tomatoes, avocado wedges, gherkins and caper berries, to serve

Heat your oven to 120°C. Place the chips in a large saucepan and pour in about 8 cups (2 litres) water, until completely submerged. Add the salt and vinegar and bring to a simmer. Cook for about 15 minutes, or until the chips are tender, but still retain their shape. Drain gently and spread out in a single layer on a baking tray lined with a tea towel. Bake for 15 minutes, or until dry. Keep uncovered on the bench until ready to fry.

To make the batter, place the flour in a large bowl and pour in the beer, lightly whisking until just combined. You don't want to over-whisk the batter – a few lumps are fine.

Pour the oil into a wok or large heavy-based saucepan and heat to 200°C. In batches, deep-fry the chips for 2 minutes. Transfer to a wire rack and drain for at least 10 minutes.

Return the chips to the hot oil for a further 4 minutes, or until golden brown, then remove and drain. You can keep the chips warm in the oven while you cook the fish.

Reduce the heat of the oil to 180°C. Coat the fish fillets in the batter, shaking off any excess. In batches, deep-fry the fish fillets for 2–3 minutes, or until golden brown and just cooked through. Drain well on a wire rack set inside a tray.

Season the fish and chips with sea salt. Serve immediately with tartare sauce, lemon wedges and your crudité salad ingredients.

NOTE Adding vinegar to the water in which the chips are boiled helps them retain their shape during boiling. Don't try to overcomplicate beer batter by adding eggs, herbs and spices, or any fancy ingredients. A cup and a half of self-raising flour and a bottle of chilled beer is all you need.

Laying a foil-wrapped brick on top of a butterflied chicken on a barbecue keeps the chicken flat so it cooks evenly, and also traps in heat, allowing it to cook faster. The result is a more tender and juicy barbecued bird.

Instead of lemon myrtle, try this recipe with lemongrass or, for something a little more traditional, rosemary, thyme and lemon.

BARBECUED BRICK CHICKEN WITH LEMON MYRTLE

PREPARATION 20 MINUTES + BARBECUE HEATING
COOKING 50 MINUTES
SERVES 4

1.6 kg whole chicken

1 tablespoon dried lemon myrtle or 2 lemongrass stems (white part very finely chopped)

⅓ cup (80 ml) olive oil

sea salt flakes, for seasoning

a small branch of fresh lemon myrtle or 2 cups soaked oak woodchips (optional)

YOGHURT AÏOLI

5 garlic cloves, crushed

1 teaspoon salt

2 egg yolks

1 cup (250 ml) olive oil

2 tablespoons Greek-style yoghurt

Heat a charcoal kettle barbecue with offset heat to 180°C. To butterfly the chicken, remove the backbone by cutting along each side with strong scissors or poultry shears, then press down on the breast to flatten the bird.

Combine the dried lemon myrtle and oil in a bowl and season with salt flakes. Rub the lemon myrtle marinade over and underneath the chicken skin. Season the chicken well with more salt flakes.

Wrap a brick with foil, ensuring it is well covered. Place the chicken, skin side down, onto the off-heat side of the barbecue, drizzling any excess marinade over the bird. Place the brick on top to flatten the chicken. Cover with a lid and let the chicken roast for 30 minutes.

Remove the brick, turn the chicken over and add the lemon myrtle branch or oak chips to the fire, if using. Roast for a further 15–20 minutes, or until cooked through. Remove the chicken from the barbecue and set aside for 10 minutes to rest.

While the chicken is resting, make the yoghurt aïoli. In a small food processor, blend the garlic, salt and egg yolks to a paste. Pour in the oil a little a time, mixing constantly until the mixture is thick and emulsified. Stir the yoghurt through and transfer the aïoli to a bowl.

Serve the chicken with the aïoli.

NOTE If you're going to the effort of firing up a barbecue kettle, I recommend cooking at least two birds. It takes no more effort than cooking one and the succulent chicken is great eaten cold.

The quality of prawns comes down to two main factors: clean estuarial waters without pollution from either the land or the sea, and fishermen who know how to handle their catch. Australian prawns are excellent quality, especially the ones from South Australia's Spencer Gulf, and the northern New South Wales coastal town of Yamba.

GRILLED PRAWNS
WITH FENNEL & SALTY LIME

PREPARATION 10 MINUTES
COOKING 10 MINUTES
SERVES 2

12 raw extra-large Yamba prawns or other high-quality, ethically sourced prawns, unpeeled

1 tablespoon olive oil

1 dried red chilli

1 tablespoon sea salt flakes

½ teaspoon fennel seeds

¼ teaspoon coriander seeds

¼ teaspoon black peppercorns

juice of 2 limes

Remove the intestines from the prawns by either pulling them out with a skewer between the plates of the shell, or by splitting down the back of each prawn with a sharp knife. Brush each prawn with a little oil.

Take a sheet of foil and fold it in half. Place the dried chilli on top, along with the salt flakes, fennel and coriander seeds, and peppercorns. Fold the foil around the spices, into an enclosed package.

Heat a barbecue grill to medium heat and toast the package of spices for about 5 minutes. Grill the prawns for 2–3 minutes on each side, or until just cooked through, then transfer to a serving plate.

Grind the toasted spices to a coarse powder using a mortar and pestle and transfer to a small dish. To eat, mix the lime juice with the ground spices and dip the prawns into the salty lime and spice mixture.

NOTE Seafood cooked in the shell will always have more flavour than if it's peeled before cooking. Whether grilling, boiling or frying, I always try to cook prawns, lobsters, crabs and any other shellfish as whole as possible.

This version of paella uses ingredients gathered along the Pacific Coast of northern New South Wales, but also follows the classic touchpoints that make a traditional Valencian paella great: cook the *sofrito* (the mix of capsicum, onion, garlic and tomato) low and slow to draw the flavours out of the aromatics; use a flavourful stock; and make sure you wait for the crackling sound of the *socarrat* (the crispy base) forming at the bottom of the pan. Good paella is all about technique.

PACIFIC PAELLA

PREPARATION 20 MINUTES
COOKING 45 MINUTES
SERVES 6

¼ cup (60 ml) olive oil

1 red capsicum, chopped

1 onion, roughly chopped

2 garlic cloves, finely chopped

2 tomatoes, halved and coarsely grated, skins discarded

300 g free-range pork belly, cut into 2.5 cm pieces

300 g boneless chicken thigh pieces, skin on, cut into 2.5 cm pieces

4 thyme sprigs

2 bay leaves

1 tablespoon smoked paprika

1¾ cups (435 ml) white wine

4 cups (1 litre) unsalted chicken or fish stock

a pinch of saffron threads

2¼ cups (500 g) paella rice (see Note)

6 raw large prawns

1 cup (155 g) frozen peas, thawed in cold water and drained

6 large Pacific oysters, scrubbed clean and shucked, on the half shell

chopped parsley, to garnish

lemon wedges, to serve

Place a paella pan or wide frying pan over medium heat and pour in the oil. Add the capsicum, onion and garlic and cook for 5 minutes, stirring frequently until fragrant. Add the tomato, season with salt and stir to combine. Reduce the heat to medium–low and cook for 10 minutes, or until reduced and slightly caramelised, stirring frequently.

Add the pork and chicken and cook for 3 minutes, or until lightly browned. Add the thyme sprigs, bay leaves and paprika, stirring well to combine.

Deglaze the pan with the wine, using a wooden spoon to scrape up any brown 'fond' that has formed on the bottom of the pan. ('Fond' is the term for the burnt or browned crust in the bottom of a pan after frying.) Stir in the stock and saffron and bring to a simmer. Scatter the rice evenly around the pan, making sure none of it is sitting above the surface of the stock. Season with salt and bring to a simmer.

Once the rice starts to swell and just touch the surface of the liquid, press the prawns into the rice. Reduce the heat to low and cook for about 20 minutes, until you can hear the crackling sound of the rice toasting on the base of the pan.

Cook for a further 3 minutes, then scatter the peas around the pan and place the oysters on top, shell side down, pushing them into the rice. Turn off the heat, cover the pan with a damp tea towel and leave to stand for 10 minutes, or until the oysters have warmed through. Serve the paella scattered with parsley and lemon wedges.

NOTE Calasparra and bomba rices are Japonica varieties of rice traditionally used for making paella in Spain, but I use koshihikari rice (sometimes called sushi rice) as it's another Japonica variety that's grown in Australia, and also makes a great paella.

Salt and pepper squid might well be Australia's national dish. I can hardly think of another that is so widely available, from pubs to cafes, bistros and restaurants. While the resilient squid can be simply tossed in a little flour, more delicate seafood, such as Queensland's extraordinary Moreton Bay bug, may need a light, crispy batter to protect it from the ravages of boiling oil.

SALT & PEPPER MORETON BAY BUGS

PREPARATION 10 MINUTES
COOKING 10 MINUTES
SERVES 6 AS PART OF A
SHARED MEAL

8 cups (2 litres) canola or sunflower oil, for deep-frying

100 g potato flour

½ cup (125 ml) chilled soda water

2 egg whites

6 raw Moreton Bay bugs, peeled, intestinal tract removed, halved lengthways

2 cm piece of fresh ginger, peeled and thinly sliced

2 garlic cloves, roughly chopped

2 long red chillies, thinly sliced on an angle

2 spring onions, thinly sliced on an angle

1 teaspoon sea salt flakes

1 teaspoon freshly ground black peppercorns

1 tablespoon roasted macadamia nuts (optional)

Half-fill a large wok with the oil and heat to 175°C.

Place the potato flour in a large bowl. Whisk in the soda water until combined. In a separate bowl, whisk the egg whites until frothy, then add to the potato flour mixture and whisk until combined.

In two batches, dip the bugs into the batter, allowing any excess to drain off. Deep-fry the bugs for about 3 minutes, or until light golden and almost cooked through. Drain well on a wire rack set inside a tray.

Remove the oil from the wok, leaving about 1 tablespoon, and reheat the wok over medium–high heat. Add the ginger, then the garlic, chilli and spring onion. Toss until well combined and fragrant.

Return the bugs to the wok and toss to combine. Add the sea salt flakes and pepper, tossing the bugs until they are well coated.

Transfer the bug mixture to a platter. Serve immediately, using a rasp grater to grate the nuts over, if using.

NOTE To extract the meat from the raw bugs, insert your thumb into the notch between the head and the tail and, grasping the tail, twist to remove it. Hold the bug 'belly' of the shell up in your hand and squeeze firmly to crack the 'ribs' of the shell, then placing your thumbs along the 'ribs', break open the tail and remove the meat.

Given it comes from such a big, ungainly creature, camel meat is surprisingly delicate, with a flavour similar to veal. It's also very lean, so mixing in some hump fat is necessary to produce a good burger patty. You can find camel meat at some specialty butchers, but if that all sounds a bit difficult you can make these burgers with cheap minced beef.

BANH-MI CAMEL BURGERS

PREPARATION 20 MINUTES +
40 MINUTES PICKLING
COOKING 10 MINUTES
SERVES 4

750 g fatty minced camel
(25% hump fat)

2 teaspoons salt

2 red radishes, very
thinly sliced

1 small Lebanese cucumber,
peeled at intervals, then
very thinly sliced

½ red onion, very
thinly sliced

½ cup mint leaves

½ cup coriander leaves

oil, for brushing

4 burger buns, halved

Japanese mayonnaise,
to serve

sriracha chilli sauce, to serve

VIETNAMESE DO CHUA PICKLE

1 small daikon (white
radish), peeled and cut
into very thin matchsticks

1 carrot, cut into very
thin matchsticks

1 tablespoon sea salt flakes

1 cup (250 ml) white
vinegar

¼ cup (55 g) white
granulated sugar

To make the Vietnamese pickle, mix the daikon, carrot and salt flakes in a bowl until well combined, then set aside for 10 minutes. In a jug, combine the vinegar and sugar, pour in 1 cup (250 ml) water and stir until dissolved. Drain the carrot and daikon and squeeze out as much liquid as possible, then add the pickling liquid, stirring to combine. Chill in the fridge for at least 30 minutes.

Place the camel meat in a large bowl, sprinkle with the salt and mix well to combine. Mould the mixture into four burger patties and place on a tray. Chill in the fridge for 20 minutes.

Make a simple herb salad by tossing the radish, cucumber, onion and herbs in a bowl until well combined.

Heat a grill plate or frying pan over high heat and brush with oil. Cook the burgers for about 4 minutes each side, or until cooked to your liking.

Lightly toast the cut sides of the buns, then spread with mayonnaise and sriracha. Add the burgers to the bottom halves, then top with the pickle and herb salad. Place the lids on top, secure each burger with a skewer if desired and serve.

NOTE If you're making these burgers – or any burgers, really – with minced beef, I recommend buying the cheapest mince from your butcher or supermarket, as it tends to have the highest fat content. A good fat percentage is necessary to make a good, juicy burger. I never add 'fillers' like herbs, breadcrumbs, onion or eggs to my burger patties. What's the point?

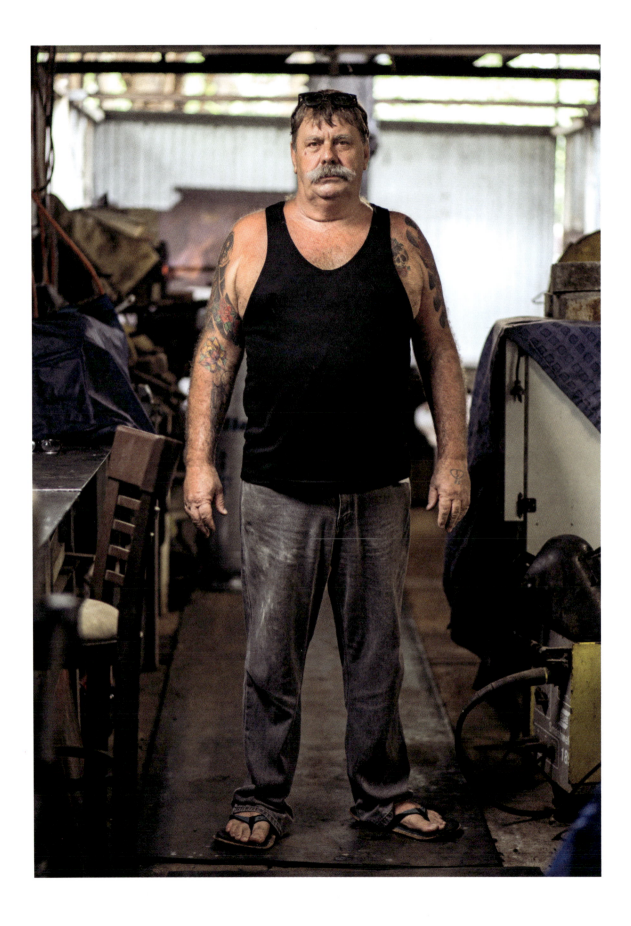

STEVE SUNK

I FIRST MET STEVE OUT IN THE BACK OF BEYOND, IN A TOWN CALLED
HUMPTY DOO, A LITTLE SOUTH OF DARWIN IN THE NORTHERN TERRITORY.
IF YOU JUDGED STEVE'S BOOK BY ITS COVER, YOU'D THINK HE'D BE
THE KIND OF GUY TO ROUGH YOU UP IN A COUNTRY PUB FOR
LOOKING AT HIM FUNNY.

But the reality is beautifully different. A big-hearted character
with an easy laugh, Steve spends much of his time with
remote Indigenous communities in the Territory teaching
nutrition, hygiene and life skills through cooking. Although the
communities are usually suspicious of outsiders, Steve spends
weeks at a time with them, accepted through decades of
building strong friendships.

I took this photo in his shed, which doubles as his forge and
foundry. He made me a beautiful set of knives with steel from
old twisted shipping cables, and handles carved from camel
bones. My favourite is a small, heavy boning knife I've dubbed
'The Croc Knife'. It might be the only handmade crocodile-
boning knife in the world.

Steve hammers the steel with an old hydraulic rock crusher he
found abandoned in a field in South Australia. It sprays sparks of
white-hot metal with every strike, which doesn't seem to bother
Steve much, despite his singlet and thongs.

After the knives were made Steve put me to work, showing me
how to fillet a crocodile tail and find the bolts of pungent fat
that run down each fillet, which taint the flavour of the meat
if not removed.

My set of knives from Steve – complete with its one-of-a-kind
'Croc Knife' – is still one of my favourite gifts from all of my
travels, and every time I use it I'm reminded of big Steve and
his big heart.

Wrapping fish in paperbark protects it and holds in moisture, and also provides a distinct and delicious smoky flavour that is fantastic with meaty barramundi just thrown on some hot coals. When such perfect ingredients are found all around, it's no wonder barbecues are Australia's national pastime.

PAPERBARK-WRAPPED BARRAMUNDI WITH SALTBUSH WILD RICE

PREPARATION 10 MINUTES +
1 HOUR SOAKING
COOKING 30 MINUTES
SERVES 6–8

1.8 kg whole barramundi, cleaned

60 ml (¼ cup) olive oil, plus extra for drizzling

6 spring onions, white and light green parts thinly sliced, dark green parts reserved

3 lemons, 1 sliced, the others cut into wedges

1 bunch dill, roughly chopped, stems reserved

1 large sheet of paperbark (see Notes)

3 garlic cloves, thinly sliced

3 cups (135 g) picked saltbush or baby English spinach, roughly chopped

1 cup (200 g) jasmine rice, rinsed and drained

1 cup (190 g) wild rice or Thai red rice (see Notes), soaked in cold water for 1 hour, then drained

To prepare the fish, pat dry well with paper towel. You don't need to scale the fish as you can remove the entire skin and scales later. Drizzle the fish cavity with a little oil and season with salt. Stuff the cavity with the green parts of the spring onion. Add the lemon slices and dill stems. Wrap the fish in the paperbark, then tie up with string, or wrap with foil to enclose.

Heat a hot plate or barbecue to medium heat. Cook the fish for 15 minutes on each side.

To prepare the rice, heat a saucepan over medium heat and add the oil. Cook the garlic and remaining spring onion bits for 2 minutes, or until slightly softened. Add the saltbush or spinach and cook for about 2 minutes, stirring regularly. Add the rice, stir to coat in the oil, and season with salt. Add 3 cups (750 ml) cold water and bring to the boil. Continue to boil until the water reaches the top of the rice. Reduce the heat to very low and cover with a lid. Cook the rice for 15 minutes, or until tender. Turn off the heat and keep covered for 10 minutes, then uncover and fluff the rice with the cutting motion of a spatula. Allow to stand uncovered for a further 5 minutes. Stir in most of the dill, squeeze in some lemon juice and season with a little salt.

Carefully unwrap the fish, then remove and discard the skin, along with the scales. Divide the rice among bowls and top with the barramundi flesh and remaining dill. Serve with the lemon wedges.

NOTES Paperbark is available from native ingredient suppliers or, if you have paperbark trees growing locally, just head out into the bush and grab some yourself. If you can't get paperbark, just use a double layer of aluminium foil.

Australian wild rice can be extremely difficult to find, as it is not a commercially produced crop. Its taste, shape and properties are very similar to Thai red rice, so that makes a great substitute.

I was a little surprised that this turned out to be one of the most popular recipes in all the seasons of *Destination Flavour*. Not because it doesn't taste good – quite the contrary, it sent the crew into absolute raptures when we made it – but because it was just one part of a more elaborate ploughman's lunch, and so I thought people might have missed it. It still makes a great ploughman's, but you could also try it with a salad for dinner. However you choose to eat it, here it is, standing alone and tall in all its glory.

SALT-CRUST PORK BELLY

PREPARATION 20 MINUTES +
30 MINUTES RESTING
COOKING 3 HOURS
SERVES 6–8

2 tablespoons fennel seeds

1 tablespoon black
   peppercorns

1.5–2 kg skinless, boneless
   pork belly

SALT CRUST

4 cups (600 g) plain flour

500 g cooking salt

Heat your oven to 180°C. In a large frying pan, toast the fennel seeds and peppercorns for about 3 minutes, or until fragrant (you don't need to add any oil). Grind the spices to a coarse powder using a mortar and pestle.

Return the frying pan to high heat and sear the pork belly until well browned on all sides. Set aside to cool.

For the salt crust, combine the flour, salt and 1 cup (250 ml) water in a large bowl and mix to a rough dough. Turn the dough out onto a lightly floured surface and knead until smooth. Roll the dough out into a large sheet, about 5 mm thick and big enough to fully encase the pork.

Scatter half the spice mixture onto the centre of the dough and place the pork on top, fat side down. Rub the remaining spice mixture all over the pork. Fold the dough over to encase the pork, then seal the edges by pressing together firmly, ensuring there are no holes.

Place the pork in a large roasting tin, seam side down. Transfer to the oven and bake for 3 hours.

Remove from the oven and allow to rest for at least 30 minutes.

When you're ready to eat, break open the crust and discard it. Slice the pork thickly to serve.

NOTE This is one of my go-to recipes for picnics. The fully enclosed crust makes it very easy to transport, but also keeps the meat warm for hours. Some cheese, a few pickles, some crudités and apple wedges and it's a perfect ploughman's.

If you've never baked a loaf in your life, this focaccia is a great place to start. It's incredibly easy to make and you don't have to worry about tending sourdough starters, hydration percentages or cold-proofing. Just throw the ingredients together and I promise it'll come out okay at the end of the day.

GRAPE & ROSEMARY FOCACCIA

PREPARATION 15 MINUTES +
1 HOUR 20 MINUTES PROVING
COOKING 25 MINUTES
SERVES 4–6

4 cups (600 g) strong flour, plus extra for dusting

2 teaspoons instant dried yeast

2 teaspoons sea salt flakes

¼ cup (60 ml) extra-virgin olive oil, plus extra for greasing, drizzling and dipping

200 g seedless red grapes, halved if large

¼ cup rosemary sprigs

chunks of good-quality hard cheese (such as Parmigiano Reggiano), to serve

Combine the flour, yeast and 1 teaspoon of the salt flakes in a large bowl and stir to combine. In a separate bowl or jug, combine the oil with 400 ml lukewarm water. Make a well in the centre of the flour mixture. Gradually add the oil mixture to the dry ingredients, stirring with a fork until the dough forms a shaggy ball.

Tip the dough out onto a lightly floured board or bench and knead for about 5 minutes, or until smooth and elastic. Place the dough into a greased bowl and roll it around to coat in the oil. Cover with a tea towel and allow the dough to prove in a warm, draught-free place for 1 hour, or until doubled in size.

Generously grease a 20 cm × 30 cm baking tin. Punch down the dough, then press it into the pan, pressing into the dough with your fingertips to leave small indentations. Push the grapes and rosemary sprigs into the dough, then drizzle generously with more olive oil and scatter with the remaining salt.

Heat your oven to 200°C. Meanwhile, allow the dough to prove for a further 20 minutes.

Bake the focaccia for 25 minutes, or until golden and cooked through. Serve with chunks of cheese, and good olive oil for dipping.

NOTE Don't skimp on the olive oil here, particularly when drizzling it over the focaccia prior to baking. It will ensure the top gets crisp and brown.

This page: Catching and cooking barramundi, Edith Falls, Northern Territory
Opposite: A short break in the ride, outside Milawa, Victoria

On the day we visited Holy Goat Cheese in Central Victoria, Ann-Marie Monda and Carla Meurs showed us around their acclaimed cheesery. We milked goats and made cheese together, learning the names of each animal and tracing their lineage. Then we sat down to a lovely long lunch … of goat.

Carla and Ann-Marie are mainly vegetarian, but they do eat the male goats that aren't needed for a milk and cheese operation. Waste not, want not.

ROAST PUMPKIN WITH FENNEL SEED, CURRY LEAF & GOAT'S CHEESE

PREPARATION 10 MINUTES
COOKING 45 MINUTES
SERVES 6 AS A SIDE DISH

½ small Japanese or
   Kent pumpkin

6 eschalots

2 tablespoons olive oil

1 tablespoon sherry vinegar

1 teaspoon honey

1 teaspoon fennel seeds

a handful of curry leaves

125 g goat's cheese

Heat your oven to 180°C. Remove the seeds from the pumpkin and chop it into thick crescents; you don't need to peel it. Peel the eschalots, leaving them whole.

In a large bowl, mix together the oil, vinegar, honey, fennel seeds and curry leaves until combined. Gently toss the pumpkin and eschalots through the mixture, then transfer to a large roasting tin. Season well with salt.

Roast for 45 minutes, or until the eschalots and pumpkin are well caramelised.

Transfer to a serving plate and crumble the goat's cheese over the top. Grind some black pepper over and serve.

NOTE This recipe uses the common feta-style soft goat's cheese, but you can use any type you prefer. It's particularly good with a few slices of Holy Goat's award-winning La Luna, a soft-textured yeast rind cheese, warmed by adding it in the last 10 minutes of roasting, and some fresh goat's curd dotted on top.

This exotic-sounding ice cream is actually very simple to make. A classic crème anglaise is sweetened and flavoured with jam. This is a great way to put interesting jams to work, if you get a bit bored with spreading them on toast or scones. I made this with a native kakadu plum jam made by an Indigenous community in northern Western Australia. Kakadu plum (also called *gubinge*) tastes a bit like a sour apple crossed with an apricot. It's delicious.

KAKADU PLUM JAM ICE CREAM

PREPARATION 15 MINUTES + AT LEAST 2 HOURS FREEZING
COOKING 15 MINUTES
MAKES 4 CUPS (1 LITRE)

2 cups (500 ml) milk

1 cup (250 ml) pouring cream

80 g caster sugar

6 egg yolks

½ cup (160 g) Kakadu plum jam, or any other kind of jam

Combine the milk and cream in a saucepan and bring to a low simmer over medium heat.

Whisk the sugar and egg yolks in a large, heatproof bowl until thick and pale.

Gradually whisk the hot milk mixture into the egg mixture until well combined.

Return the mixture to the saucepan and place over medium–low heat for a few minutes, stirring with a spatula and scraping the sides of the saucepan until the mixture coats the back of the spatula.

Add the jam to a large bowl. Strain the crème anglaise into the bowl through a fine sieve and whisk until well combined. Refrigerate until cold (about 30 minutes). Transfer the cooled mixture into an ice-cream machine and churn according to the manufacturer's instructions.

Transfer the churned mixture to a freezer-proof container and freeze for at least 2 hours, or until firm.

NOTE If you don't have an ice-cream maker you can just place the bowl of jam and crème anglaise mixture directly into the freezer and whisk it every 30 minutes for about 2–3 hours until it becomes too thick to whisk, then let it continue to freeze until firm.

Sometimes dishes just fall into your lap. On the day I visited Garrie and Giuliana Vincenti on their peach farm in Western Australia I had set out to make a classic Peach Melba – a dish of poached peaches, raspberry coulis and vanilla ice cream made by the famed chef Auguste Escoffier at the Savoy Hotel in London to honour Australian soprano Dame Nellie Melba back in 1893. But filming in the Australian summer heat, our ice cream melted and our raspberries were looking a bit tired, so I decided to take a leaf from Garrie and Giuliana's Italian heritage instead. I think Giuliana was a bit embarrassed about having a dish named after her, but the name seemed appropriate.

PEACH GIULIANA

PREPARATION 30 MINUTES + 4 HOURS FREEZING
COOKING 45 MINUTES
SERVES 6

1½ cups (375 ml) sparkling wine or Prosecco

¾ cup (170 g) caster sugar

6 thyme sprigs, plus extra to garnish

3 firm, ripe white or yellow peaches, halved, stones removed

⅓ cup (110 g) mascarpone

RASPBERRY GRANITA

2 cups (250 g) raspberries

1 cup (250 ml) peach poaching liquor (from above)

ZABAGLIONE

4 egg yolks

⅓ cup (75 g) caster sugar

⅓ cup (80 ml) sparkling wine or Prosecco

To poach the peaches, add the wine, sugar and thyme sprigs to a large saucepan. Pour in 2 cups (500 ml) water and bring to the boil, stirring to dissolve the sugar. Cook for 5 minutes, then add the peach halves and reduce the heat to medium–low. Cover the surface with a cartouche. Simmer for a further 5 minutes, or until the peaches are tender.

Remove the peaches from the poaching liquid, reserving 1 cup (250 ml) of the liquid for the granita. Refrigerate the peaches and reserved poaching liquid. Once the peaches are cool enough to handle, slip off their skins. Pour the chilled poaching liquid over the peaches and return to the fridge until ready to serve.

To make the granita, purée the raspberries in a food processor or blender with 1 cup (250 ml) of the poaching liquid. Pour the mixture into a shallow tray and freeze for 4 hours, or until frozen solid.

Whip the mascarpone until lightly aerated. Chill until ready to serve.

For the zabaglione, whisk the egg yolks and sugar in a heatproof bowl placed over a saucepan of barely simmering water. Add the wine and continue to whisk over the heat for 15 minutes, or until the mixture has tripled in size and is very thick and fluffy. Check the bottom of the bowl while you are whisking; it should be warm but not too hot to touch (see Notes). Remove from the heat and continue to beat for a further 5 minutes, or until the mixture has cooled.

To serve, scrape the granita with a fork to create light, fluffy crystals. Spoon a bit of whipped mascarpone into the base of six serving glasses, then add a generous amount of zabaglione. Top with a spoonful of granita, garnish with a sprig of thyme and serve with a peach half. Serve immediately.

NOTES A cartouche is a piece of greaseproof paper placed directly onto the surface of the simmering liquid.

Don't overheat your whisking bowl when making zabaglione (or sabayon, as the French call it). Keep touching the bottom of the bowl regularly throughout the whisking – if it's too hot to touch, you run the risk of overheating the mixture, which will make it 'eggy' and grainy. Also make sure the base of the bowl isn't sitting in the hot water.

A good pavlova is hands-down my favourite cake, if you can call it that – and the trick to making a good one is very simple actually. The main problems with a pavlova are caused by an unstable meringue, and the way to stabilise it is by making sure the sugar is completely dissolved, and also by adding a little acid (such as cream of tartar or vinegar) to the mix. Follow this method and you'll have a successful pav every time.

GOLDEN CROWN PAVLOVA

PREPARATION 30 MINUTES + AT LEAST 3 HOURS COOLING
COOKING 1½ HOURS
SERVES 6–8

6 egg whites

1½ cups (330 g) caster sugar

1 tablespoon cornflour

¼ teaspoon cream of tartar

a pinch of salt

300 ml thickened cream

½ teaspoon natural vanilla extract

150 g thick coconut yoghurt

an assortment of chopped or sliced golden and yellow fruits to top the pavlova, such as feijoa, yellow nectarine, banana, mango, papaya and passionfruit

SPUN SUGAR

1 cup (220 g) sugar

Heat your oven to 110°C. Whisk the egg whites to soft peaks in the bowl of a stand mixer. Sprinkle in the caster sugar a tablespoon at a time and continue to beat until glossy. About halfway through adding the sugar, stir the cornflour, cream of tartar and salt into the sugar, then continue adding to the egg white mixture. Beat for a further 10 minutes after all the sugar has been added. The whole process should take about 15–20 minutes, and you should not be able to feel any grains of sugar when you rub the mixture between your fingers.

Line a baking tray with a sheet of baking paper and spread the meringue on the baking paper in a rough cake shape. If you keep adding meringue to the centre and pushing it down, the pavlova will form an attractive natural edge.

Place in the oven and bake for 90 minutes, then turn off the oven, allowing the pavlova to cool without opening the door for at least 3 hours, but preferably overnight.

For the spun sugar, place the sugar in a small saucepan with 2 tablespoons cold water and swirl the pan to mix. Place over medium–high heat and swirl occasionally until the mixture forms a dark golden caramel. Remove from the heat and allow to cool slightly. Dip two forks into the caramel and draw the forks away. As the mixture cools it will form long threads as the forks are drawn away; at this point the sugar is ready to be spun. Repeatedly 'cast' the sugar over a large metal bowl to form long threads supported by the edges of the bowl. Gather the threads together into a crown shape.

Whip the cream to soft peaks with the vanilla, then mix the yoghurt through.

Dollop the cream and yoghurt mixture onto the pavlova and top with your assortment of fruits. Top with the crown of spun sugar.

NOTE Some people warn about over-whipping the meringue but, in reality, once the sugar has been added, that is very difficult to do. However, the sugar stabilises the meringue, so you need to ensure it has been fully dissolved when whipping the egg whites.

Cooking in interesting locations is one of the most exciting, and at the same time most difficult, things about making a series like *Destination Flavour*. As it is for most people, cooking in my own kitchen is well within my comfort zone, but take the same dishes out into the elements and all of a sudden you have to start thinking a bit more tactically. At home I make my shortcrust pastry with a food processor, but when you're standing in the middle of a berry patch you need to come up with alternative ways to do things. Grating the frozen butter to make the pastry for these tarts worked a treat.

BLACKBERRY PICNIC TARTS

PREPARATION 10 MINUTES +
20 MINUTES CHILLING
COOKING 30 MINUTES
MAKES 12

2⅓ cups (300 g) fresh
    blackberries

2 tablespoons caster sugar

1½ tablespoons cornflour

300 ml thickened cream

2 tablespoons icing sugar

SHORTCRUST PASTRY

⅔ cup (100 g) plain flour

65 g caster sugar

½ cup (125 g) very cold or
    frozen unsalted butter

1 egg yolk

To make the pastry, combine the flour and sugar in a large bowl. Working quickly, grate the butter into the bowl and rub the butter into the flour mixture until it resembles breadcrumbs. Add the egg yolk and, if necessary, a teaspoon or two of cold water to bring the dough together.

Push a small amount of dough into each hole of a standard 12-hole non-stick muffin tin and press around the sides to line it evenly. Refrigerate for 20 minutes, or until firm.

Heat your oven to 180°C.

Place the berries in a bowl and stir in the caster sugar. Lightly crush the berries to release their juices, then stir the cornflour through. Spoon the mixture into the tart cases, then bake for 25–30 minutes, or until the pastry is golden. Allow to cool.

Whip the cream to soft peaks, then serve the picnic tarts topped with the cream and a dusting of icing sugar.

NOTE It's easy to whip cream at home, but if you're bringing these tarts to a picnic just pour the cream into a large jar of at least 450 ml capacity and keep it chilled along with your drinks. When ready to serve, shake the jar for about 5 minutes, or until the cream is aerated and 'whipped'.

CHINA

Beyond its borders, Chinese food is possibly the most misunderstood in the entire world. To even call it 'Chinese food' is wholly inadequate. An enormous country with thousands of years of history, China is incredibly regional, with hundreds of individual dialects and cuisines that can vary over distances of even just a few kilometres.

For centuries, Chinese gourmets have referred to the 'eight great regional cuisines' of China – Anhui, Fujian, Guangdong, Hunan, Jiangsu, Shandong, Sichuan and Zhejiang – each with their individual characteristics and specialties. For *Destination Flavour China*, we chose to tell the story of Chinese food through these regions. My hope was that, through doing so, we might shed some light onto what is both the most mysterious and most influential cuisine humankind has ever seen. →

China is the birthplace of so many foods we regard as common today: noodles (their history in China pre-dates pasta in the West by more than 500 years), tea, cured meats (first recorded in China an astounding 7000 years ago) and even tomato sauce. The world 'ketchup' is based on the Hokkien *kê-tsiap*, a savoury fermented fish sauce popular in Fujian province that was the precursor of the tomato-based sauce we see today.

But despite its millennia of history, perhaps the most astonishing thing about Chinese food is just how relevant it remains today. You can get a Chinese meal in more places around the world than any other cuisine. It was carried to every part of the globe by the industriousness of a fifty million–strong overseas Chinese diaspora seeking their fortunes abroad but still holding tightly to their culture and traditions.

As China's economy continues to develop faster than any nation's in history, the prominence and influence of Chinese cuisine can only increase.

For me, the most confronting part of my exploration into Chinese food was how personal it became. My father's family originated on Hainan island in the south of China, and my mother has lived in Beijing for twenty-five years. While growing up in Australia, I considered myself a Chinese kid, but I only set foot in China for the first time when I was fourteen, and speak broken Mandarin at best. Few Chinese would consider me 'Chinese' at all.

And yet with every step of my travels through the country, I could feel my connection to my family heritage growing stronger and stronger.

Pages 64–5: Tiananmen Square and the Forbidden City, Beijing
Top left: Longjing tea fields, Zhejiang
Top right: Traditional rapeseed oil production, Fu'e County, Anhui
Bottom left: A mountain village in Nanjing County, Fujian
Bottom middle: Tofu makers Niu Zhong Ming and Du Shu Xia, Anhui
Bottom right: Manchurian-style yum cha, Beijing

In the West, our understanding of wok cooking has been hampered by two long-persisting myths. The first is that a wok is a big pot. While it might be large in size, the utility of a wok is not that you can fit a lot into it, but rather that its shape allows you to cook very small amounts of food efficiently, letting you make multiple dishes in succession. The second is that stir-fried ingredients are added into a wok in the order of the time they take to cook. The reality is that aromatic ingredients like ginger and garlic are added first to flavour the oil, and ingredients that cook at different rates are cooked separately, then combined in the wok at the end.

With this in mind, trying to pile enough food to feed a whole family into one wok is a recipe for failure. Instead of making one big stir-fry of eight ingredients, make four small stir-fries of two main ingredients each. They'll taste a lot better.

STIR-FRIED BAMBOO SHOOTS & CURED HAM

PREPARATION 10 MINUTES
COOKING 5 MINUTES
SERVES 2–4 AS PART OF
A SHARED MEAL

2 tablespoons vegetable oil, approximately

2 cm piece of fresh ginger, peeled and shredded

85 g cured pork belly, or 50 g pancetta, thinly sliced

2 fresh bamboo shoots, peeled and sliced, or 1½ cups (375 g) bamboo shoot pieces

¼ cup (60 ml) Anhui yellow wine, or 2 tablespoons shaoxing wine

a pinch of sugar

2 green garlic shoots (or 2 garlic cloves and 2 thick spring onions)

1 large fresh chilli

1 teaspoon cornflour, mixed to a slurry with 2 tablespoons water or stock (if needed)

Heat a wok over medium–high heat and add the oil. Add the ginger and fry for about 30 seconds, or until fragrant. Add the pork and fry for a minute or so, until the pork is browned. Remove the pork and ginger from the wok and return the wok to the heat.

Add the bamboo shoots, and a little more oil if necessary, and stir-fry for about 2 minutes. Add the wine, sugar, and a little water or stock if necessary to keep the bamboo shoots moist. Add the garlic shoots and chilli and toss to combine, then return the pork and ginger to the wok and toss well.

If necessary, thicken any liquid by adding a little cornflour slurry and tossing the wok over the heat for a minute, then remove to a serving plate and serve.

NOTE All through Anhui the local people cure their own pork in winter, which is often as simple as hanging a piece of pork in the cold, dry air and salting it every week or so. The result is a favourite ingredient in Anhui's simple stir-fried dishes. Combined with Anhui's famous bamboo shoots and a touch of wild garlic and chilli for colour, this kind of simple stir-fry is a staple dish around the region.

Red-braised pork could well be the national dish of China. For a cuisine as diverse as China's, the provinces can't even agree on a staple grain – to generalise, in the south it's rice; in the north, wheat, millet or barley – let alone a style of cooking. The one constant seems to be red-braised pork. It exists in dozens of regional cuisines, and Chairman Mao loved the dish so much that in his birthplace of Hunan province it even took his name.

CHAIRMAN MAO'S RED PORK

PREPARATION 20 MINUTES +
15 MINUTES STANDING
COOKING 1¼ HOURS
SERVES 6 AS PART OF A
SHARED MEAL

1.5 kg pork belly, bones
   removed

2 tablespoons peanut oil

½ cup (110 g) sugar
   or yellow rock sugar
   (available from Asian
   grocery stores)

1 cup (250 ml) shaoxing
   wine

¼ teaspoon salt

8 slices fresh ginger,
   lightly bruised

2 star anise

6 dried red chillies

1 piece of cassia bark
   or cinnamon

2 tablespoons soy sauce

Place the pork in a large saucepan and cover with water. Place over high heat and bring to the boil. Allow to boil for 15 minutes, then remove the pork and discard the water.

Rinse the pan and set aside. Wash the pork under running water to remove any scum, then cut into 5 cm blocks; the pork will not be cooked through.

Place the rinsed pan back over medium heat and add the oil and half the sugar. Fry the sugar until it becomes a dark caramel, then add the pork and stir to coat.

Add the shaoxing wine, salt, ginger, star anise, chillies, cassia and enough cold water to just cover the pork. Bring to a simmer, cover with a cartouche of baking paper (see Notes on page 59) and simmer for 30 minutes.

Remove the cartouche. Stir in the soy sauce, then simmer, uncovered, for a further 15–20 minutes, or until the pork is tender and the liquid slightly reduced and glossy.

Taste the liquid and adjust any seasoning if necessary.

Allow to stand for 15 minutes and reheat if needed before serving.

People in northern and western China go crazy for these skewers, particularly in summer. In Beijing, as soon as the weather warms up, tables spill out onto the streets and, outdoors in the hot night air, the locals down millions of these skewers washed down with cold beer. I've spent many a Beijing night doing just that. Their spiritual home, however, is Xinjiang province in China's far west. Out there, these skewers are like mother's milk.

XINJIANG-STYLE LAMB SKEWERS

PREPARATION 20 MINUTES
+ OVERNIGHT MARINATING +
30 MINUTES SOAKING
COOKING 5 MINUTES
SERVES 4

1.5 kg lamb forequarter
chops or lamb shoulder

3 teaspoons cumin seeds

2 teaspoons chilli powder
(preferably Korean, as it
can be a little milder)

2 teaspoons fennel seeds

1 teaspoon sichuan
peppercorns (optional)

1½ teaspoons salt

1 teaspoon soy sauce

½ teaspoon caster sugar

¼ cup (60 ml) vegetable oil

Debone the lamb and cut the meat and any fat into 2 cm pieces.

Using a mortar and pestle, grind together the cumin seeds, chilli powder, fennel seeds and peppercorns, if using, into a coarse powder. Mix the salt, soy sauce, sugar and oil through. With your hands, rub the paste all over the lamb, then cover and leave to marinate in the fridge overnight.

Thread the lamb pieces onto bamboo skewers that have been soaked in water for about 30 minutes, alternating a piece of fat after every two or three pieces of lean lamb meat.

Grill the skewers, preferably over coals on a barbecue, turning frequently for about 5 minutes, or until charred and fragrant. Serve warm.

NOTE It might take a little time to debone the lamb, but forequarter or shoulder have the best fat-to-meat ratio to keep the skewers moist.

BENYAN AND XU DU

IT TOOK JUST THIRTY MINUTES FOR BENYAN AND XU DU
TO DECIDE TO CHANGE THEIR LIVES.

They were living in the city of Huangshan with corporate jobs
as ordinary as can be – Benyan worked in telecommunications
and Xu Du in marketing at a furniture company. Around eight
years ago they took a weekend trip to Hongcun, an ancient town
in the mountains of Anhui province. They fell under its spell
immediately, and within half an hour they'd decided to buy a
600-year-old house and convert it into an inn for travellers.

They also bought a cabin in the woods outside Hongcun, and
spent two years living there while working on the inn. They now
split their time between Hongcun and their mountain hideaway.

Xu Du is an avid gardener, often collecting shoots from the
forests to propagate in her garden with its bee hives, chicken run
and overflowing jungle of beautiful plants.

Benyan is a renaissance man. He spends his time brewing
delicious, expressive beers and rice wines, writing calligraphy
and taking photographs. He's an extraordinarily intelligent and
intuitive cook, particularly of Anhui cuisine.

When I asked Benyan and Xu Du how their new life compares
to their old one, they just laughed.

'Is this heaven?' I persisted.

'Heaven is for dead people,' Benyan replied. 'This is paradise.'

Of all the thousands of tea varieties in China, Longjing (dragon well) tea is one of the most prized. It is baked by hand to a light yellow-green colour and has a nutty, herbaceous aroma. The taste is actually quite savoury, as many teas are. This dish perfectly combines the savoury characteristics of tea with the delicate sweetness of seafood.

LONGJING PRAWNS

PREPARATION 10 MINUTES + 10 MINUTES MARINATING AND STEEPING
COOKING 5 MINUTES
SERVES 6 AS PART OF A SHARED MEAL

500 g peeled raw small prawns, deveined

1 egg white, lightly beaten

½ teaspoon salt

1 teaspoon cornflour, plus a little extra mixed into a slurry with cold water (if needed)

1 tablespoon Longjing (dragon well) tea leaves or other Chinese green tea leaves

2 tablespoons vegetable oil

1 tablespoon shaoxing wine

Combine the prawns in a bowl with the egg white, salt, cornflour and 2 tablespoons water. Toss until well coated, then leave to marinate for 10 minutes.

Meanwhile, steep the tea leaves in ½ cup (125 ml) 70°C water for 5 minutes, then strain the tea, reserving the tea and leaves.

Heat a wok over medium heat and add the oil. Add the prawns and toss. Add the tea, shaoxing wine and a pinch of the steeped tea leaves and toss the prawns for about 3 minutes, depending on their size, until they are barely cooked through.

Thicken any liquid with a little extra cornflour slurry if necessary.

Serve immediately.

As the story goes (and there are many variations of it), a hungry beggar came across a chicken, but with no pot to cook it in improvised by covering it in clay and burying it in the embers of a fire. As he was cracking open the chicken, the Emperor was passing and stopped to share the meal. The Emperor was so taken with the taste that the dish was added to the menu of the imperial court. A lovely story, right?

Now, I don't believe for a minute that it's true (an emperor sharing a chicken baked in dirt with a beggar?), but I love that in China there are thousands of stories like this. Food is given its own mythology, from poetic names to elaborate legends, and every dish tells a story about the human condition.

BEGGAR'S CHICKEN

PREPARATION 15 MINUTES + OVERNIGHT MARINATING AND SOAKING
COOKING 3¾ HOURS + 20 MINUTES RESTING
SERVES 6–8 AS PART OF A SHARED MEAL

2 teaspoons salt

1 tablespoon soy sauce

1 tablespoon shaoxing wine

1 teaspoon five-spice

1.6 kg whole chicken

2 dried lotus leaves

STUFFING

8 dried lotus seeds

6 dried shiitake mushrooms

1 tablespoon vegetable oil

4 garlic cloves, chopped

1 teaspoon grated fresh ginger

100 g minced pork

1 Chinese sausage (lap cheong), sliced

½ cup preserved Tianjin cabbage (available in jars from Asian grocery stores)

15 g Chinese angelica

2 teaspoons soy sauce

2 teaspoons shaoxing wine

DOUGH CRUST

1 kg plain flour

1 cup (315 g) rock salt

1 egg, beaten

In a small bowl, combine the salt, soy sauce, shaoxing wine and five-spice, stirring to dissolve the salt. Rub the mixture all over the chicken, then cover and marinate in the fridge overnight. Soak the lotus seeds (for the stuffing) in cold water overnight.

The next day, soak the dried lotus leaves in warm water for 30 minutes, and the dried shiitake mushrooms (for the stuffing) in hot water for 20 minutes. Trim the stalks from the mushrooms and set the caps aside.

To make the stuffing, heat a wok over high heat and add the oil. Fry the garlic and ginger for about 1 minute, or until fragrant, then add the pork and Chinese sausage and fry, stirring occasionally, for about 3 minutes, until the pork is browned. Add the shiitake mushrooms, preserved cabbage, angelica, lotus seeds, soy sauce and shaoxing wine and toss to combine.

Stuff the chicken with the stuffing.

Heat your oven to 160°C.

For the dough crust, knead half the flour, half the salt and 700 ml water in an electric stand mixer fitted with a dough hook for about 5 minutes, until a smooth dough forms. Roll the dough out on a lightly floured surface to about 1 cm thick.

Repeat with the remaining flour, salt and the same quantity of water to make a second sheet of dough.

Lay the soaked lotus leaves over one piece of dough and place the chicken on top. Wrap the chicken in the leaves and secure the leaves with string.

Place the other dough sheet on top of the chicken and pinch to secure the chicken in a package without large air pockets.

Brush with the beaten egg, place in a roasting tin and bake for 3½ hours.

Remove from the oven and rest for 20 minutes, then crack open the dough and unwrap the chicken to serve.

The Great
Wall of China,
outside Beijing

Shandong chicken is usually made with a crispy-skinned deep-fried chicken, but poaching, drying and then deep-frying a chicken at home is no mean feat – and it would be a shame to only have the delicious flavour of Shandong chicken when you were prepared to jump through all those culinary hoops. This roast chicken version is much simpler, and it's a staple in our home.

SHANDONG ROAST CHICKEN

PREPARATION 20 MINUTES + OVERNIGHT MARINATING
COOKING 1 HOUR + 15 MINUTES RESTING
SERVES 6–8 AS PART OF A SHARED MEAL

1.6 kg whole free-range chicken

½ teaspoon salt

2 tablespoons dark soy sauce

2 tablespoons shaoxing wine

2 teaspoons grated fresh ginger, juice only

1 teaspoon sugar

1 tablespoon vegetable oil

SHANDONG SAUCE

¼ cup (60 ml) black vinegar

2 teaspoons soy sauce

2 teaspoons sugar

2 red bird's eye chillies, sliced

4 garlic cloves, finely chopped

1 whole coriander stalk, stem and root finely chopped, leaves reserved

Rub the chicken all over with the salt, inside and out.

In a small bowl, combine the soy sauce, shaoxing wine, ginger juice and sugar, stirring to dissolve the sugar. Rub the mixture all over the chicken, then marinate uncovered in the fridge overnight.

When ready to start cooking, heat your oven to 200°C. Brush the chicken all over with the oil, place in a roasting tin and roast for 1 hour.

Remove from the oven and rest for 15 minutes.

For the Shandong sauce, combine all the ingredients except the coriander leaves in a small bowl, stirring to dissolve the sugar. Stir in a few spoonfuls of the rendered chicken fat from the pan.

Cut the chicken into pieces and serve smothered in the Shandong sauce and scattered with the reserved coriander leaves.

This classic noodle dish is to northern China what spaghetti bolognese is to the rest of the world: a comforting home-style dish that has almost infinite variations. This simple version is the most common, but some others use different sauces (like a mixture of tian mian jiang and hoisin sauce), or add up to eight different toppings, such as raw sliced radish, salad greens and peanuts. Why not come up with your own family version of one of China's favourite dishes?

FRIED SAUCE NOODLES

PREPARATION 10 MINUTES
COOKING 10 MINUTES
SERVES 4

½ cup (125 ml) vegetable oil

2 large spring onions, finely sliced, white and green parts separated

2 garlic cloves, roughly chopped

1 teaspoon grated fresh ginger

300 g minced pork

¾ cup (185 ml) tian mian jiang (sweet bean sauce, sometimes called brown bean sauce)

1 kg thick wheat noodles, such as Japanese udon noodles

2 Lebanese cucumbers, seeded and julienned, to serve

Heat a wok over high heat and add the oil. Add the white and light green parts of the spring onion, the garlic and ginger and stir-fry for 1 minute, or until fragrant.

Add the pork and cook, stirring occasionally, for about 3 minutes, until lightly browned. Add the tian mian jiang and stir to combine. Fry for about 2 minutes, then turn off the heat.

Cook the noodles according to the packet directions and drain well, reserving about ½ cup (125 ml) of the cooking water.

Bring the sauce back to a simmer and add the reserved noodle cooking water, stirring well to combine.

Serve the noodles topped with a small amount of the pork mixture and sauce, cucumber, and a sprinkling of spring onion greens.

NOTE Literally meaning 'fried sauce noodles', the sauce for these noodles was originally deep-fried with the meat. I don't go quite that far, but using a fair bit of oil is still necessary as it takes on the flavour of the aromatics, meat and sauce. Make sure you don't skimp on the oil, as it is key to this dish.

This incredibly simple stir-fry is ubiquitous across China – so much so that it's hard to know where it originated. The secret of its popularity is its simplicity: readily available ingredients prepared quickly and frugally without fuss.

PORK WITH GREEN CAPSICUM

PREPARATION 15 MINUTES +
10 MINUTES MARINATING
COOKING 10 MINUTES
SERVES 4 AS PART OF A
SHARED MEAL

200 g lean pork shoulder,
   cut into 1.5 cm strips

2 tablespoons shaoxing
   wine

2 tablespoons soy sauce

2 teaspoons sesame oil

½ teaspoon sugar

¼ teaspoon ground
   white pepper

1 teaspoon cornflour,
   plus a little extra mixed
   into a slurry with cold
   water (if needed)

2 tablespoons vegetable oil,
   plus extra if needed

1 large green capsicum,
   cut into very thin strips

2 slices fresh ginger, bruised

4 garlic cloves, roughly
   chopped

In a bowl, combine the pork strips with the shaoxing wine, soy sauce, sesame oil, sugar, white pepper and cornflour. Mix well and set aside for 10 minutes to marinate.

Heat a wok over high heat and add the vegetable oil. Add the capsicum and cook for about 2 minutes, or until just tender, then remove from the wok.

Add a little extra oil to the wok if needed, then stir-fry the ginger and garlic for about 1 minute, or until fragrant.

Squeeze any excess marinade from the pork, reserving the marinade. Add the pork to the wok and fry for about 2 minutes, or until golden.

Return the capsicum to the wok, add the reserved marinade and toss to combine, cooking for about 1 minute to bring the dish together. Add a little water or stock if your mixture is too dry, or if needed add a little cornflour slurry to thicken the liquid to a silky sauce that coats the meat and vegetables.

Transfer to a plate and serve.

NOTE The biggest myth of wok cooking is that you add the ingredients to the wok in the order of the time they take to cook. In real Chinese wok cooking, if ingredients cook at different speeds, they are fried separately and combined in the wok at the end.

WEN XIANG ZHEN

MRS WEN LIVES IN THE VILLAGE OF XUNPU, NEAR QUANZHOU ON
FUJIAN'S COAST. EVERY MORNING THE MEN OF XUNPU HEAD OUT
FISHING, WHILE THE WOMEN HUNT FOR OYSTERS.

XunPu's a beautiful place. Its traditional houses have walls made
from oyster shells, and there's an easy pace of life despite being
only around half an hour from the bustle of Quanzhou.

Walk around the streets of XunPu and on every corner you'll
find ladies in their brightly coloured coats and elaborate floral
headdresses shucking thousands of tiny oysters.

The riot of colours in the women's clothes are the last vestiges of
a time when Arab sailors settled the village more than 400 years
ago. The headdresses are made from richly perfumed flowers to
mask the smell of the oysters.

I took this photo of Mrs Wen as she visited the Mazu Temple,
where the ladies of XunPu go on the fifteenth of each month to
pray and give offerings. I'd been to many temples just like this
one during my childhood.

Mazu is the goddess of sailors and she's worshipped throughout
the south of China even to Hainan Island, from where my
grandfather set sail to Malaysia nearly a hundred years ago.
Perhaps he prayed to Mazu for a safe voyage before stepping
on a boat and leaving his home forever.

The oysters that the ladies of XunPu shuck are destined for oyster
omelettes, a Fujian favourite that the sailors of the Maritime
Silk Route brought around Southeast Asia. You can find it in my
birthplace of Penang, and my mother's birthplace of Singapore.
It's my mother's favourite dish.

I shucked oysters with Mrs Wen for a while, and then we cooked
an oyster omelette together. When I ate it I thought of the last
time I'd eaten an oyster omelette with my mother, squatting
on stools in the heat of a Singapore hawker centre.

I'd never been to XunPu before, but it's amazing how food can
make even the most unfamiliar of places feel a little bit like home.

There are so many dishes in Chinese cuisine designed to show off the ostentatious expense of the ingredients, and so the status and wealth of the person serving them. Unfortunately in the past many of those expensive ingredients (such as shark fin) were expensive because of their rarity. As the focus within China and around the globe shifts to sustainability, there's a push to modernise these dishes with ethical and sustainable alternatives chosen to show the ingredient's quality rather than just its price.

This version of the classic Shandong 'Eight Immortals' is designed for just that purpose.

EIGHT IMMORTALS CROSSING THE OCEAN

PREPARATION 45 MINUTES + 30 MINUTES SOAKING + 15 MINUTES STANDING AND RESTING
COOKING 30 MINUTES
SERVES 6–8 AS PART OF A SHARED MEAL

5 dried shiitake mushrooms, soaked in 1 cup (250 ml) hot water for 30 minutes

8 asparagus spears

8 raw prawns, peeled and deveined

8 raw scallops, roe removed

1 ethically sourced reconstituted dried sea cucumber (available from Asian grocers)

1 chicken breast

1 tinned abalone, very thinly sliced

80 g prosciutto, thinly sliced

4 cups (1 litre) strong chicken stock, fish stock or a combination of each

2 tablespoons shaoxing wine

½ teaspoon salt

½ teaspoon soy sauce

3 slices fresh ginger

In a saucepan, bring about 4 cups (1 litre) salted water to a simmer. Add the shiitake mushrooms and their soaking liquid and simmer for 10 minutes, then remove the mushrooms and set them aside.

In the same pan of broth, blanch the asparagus spears for 1 minute, then refresh in iced water. Blanch the prawns and scallops separately for about 1 minute each, or until just cooked, then set aside. Simmer the sea cucumber for 2 minutes and set aside.

Finally, add the chicken breast to the broth and simmer for 5 minutes. Turn off the heat, cover with a lid and allow the chicken to stand for a further 10 minutes.

Remove the chicken from the broth, reserving the broth. Rest the chicken for 5 minutes, then thinly slice into medallions. Halve the prawns along their length, and halve the scallops horizontally. Thinly slice the shiitake mushrooms, abalone and sea cucumber. Cut the asparagus diagonally into 5 cm lengths.

Arrange the chicken, seafood, blanched vegetables and prosciutto slices, in eight separate wedges, in a shallow presentation bowl.

Meanwhile, in a separate saucepan, bring the stock to a simmer and add the shaoxing wine, salt, soy sauce and ginger. Add about 2 cups (500 ml) of the reserved blanching broth and adjust the seasoning of the soup to taste. It should be strongly savoury.

Serve the arranged ingredients and soup separately, and pour the hot soup over the arranged ingredients just before eating.

NOTE If some ingredients like sea cucumber don't appeal to you, just substitute something else. A bit of thinly sliced white fish would be delicious.

The simplicity of this Fujian dish speaks volumes of the ingenuity of true Chinese cooking. Years of 'Chinese whispers' (if you'll excuse the pun) has meant that Chinese food abroad – after travelling from China, the economic hardship of migration, and being adapted to local ingredients and local tastes in the West – has a name for being low quality, and overly oily, sweet and salty. Nothing could be further from the truth. This dish makes the most of the simplicity of two ingredients and speaks to the characteristics of Fujian cuisine, combining ingredients from the land and sea with clever, understated seasoning. The strongly savoury scallops steam slowly, passing their flavour into the softening daikon. A silky sauce ties it all together for a delicate, intelligent dish.

DAIKON STEAMED WITH DRIED SCALLOPS

PREPARATION 15 MINUTES + 30 MINUTES SOAKING
COOKING ABOUT 1 HOUR
SERVES 6–8 AS PART OF A SHARED MEAL

8–10 large dried scallops

1 daikon (white radish)

2 teaspoons vegetable oil

1 tablespoon shaoxing wine

1 teaspoon soy sauce

½ teaspoon salt, plus extra for seasoning

¼ teaspoon sugar

1 teaspoon cornflour, mixed to a slurry with a little cold water

Soak the dried scallops in 2 cups (500 ml) hot water for at least 30 minutes, then remove the scallops from the liquid, reserving the stock. Set aside.

Peel the daikon and cut into 4 cm rounds; you'll need one slice for each scallop. Season all over with salt.

With a melon baller, scoop an indentation into the centre of each piece of daikon, large enough to hold a dried scallop. Place a scallop on top of each round and place them on a heatproof plate in a steamer.

Steam for 1 hour.

Just before serving, heat a wok or small saucepan over medium heat and add the oil, shaoxing wine, soy sauce, salt, sugar and reserved scallop liquid. Simmer for 2 minutes, then taste and adjust the seasoning if necessary. While stirring the simmering liquid, pour in enough of the cornflour slurry to create a silky sauce.

Transfer the daikon rounds to a serving plate, pour the sauce over and serve immediately.

NOTE Large dried scallops can be very expensive and difficult to find. If you can only obtain small scallops, just place five or six onto each daikon round.

There's a saying in China that roughly translates as 'A meal without soup is not a meal'. It's true that soup is a staple in Chinese cooking, and a single meal might feature two or three soups at various times. Sweet soups are extremely popular in Cantonese cuisine, and a common ingredient is snow fungus (also called 'silver ear'), which is prized for its crunchy, gelatinous texture and purported health benefits.

SNOW FUNGUS & SWEET POTATO DESSERT SOUP

PREPARATION 15 MINUTES +
1 HOUR SOAKING
COOKING 1 HOUR 10 MINUTES
SERVES 4

100 g dried snow fungus
(available from Asian
grocery stores)

1 yellow-fleshed sweet
potato, peeled and cut
into large chunks

5 cm piece of fresh ginger,
peeled and bruised

150 g yellow rock sugar
(available from Asian
grocery stores)

1 tablespoon dried goji
berries

a pinch of salt

Soak the fungus in a bowl of hot water for at least 1 hour. Drain, then remove the hard base with a pair of kitchen scissors.

In a large saucepan, bring 8 cups (2 litres) water to a very low simmer. Add all the ingredients and cook at a bare simmer for 1 hour; the water should be hot enough for you to see steam rising from the pot.

Taste and adjust the seasoning. Serve warm or chilled.

NOTE I prefer these sweet soups chilled and served with a few ice cubes in them, but in China they are more often served warm.

SCANDINAVIA

One thing I love about *Destination Flavour* is that we get to take our program to the most interesting places in the world for food from one series to the next.

It wasn't so long ago that Scandinavian food would barely have registered in a discussion of 'important' cuisines. The New Nordic food movement changed all that. It's hard to really explain just how influential the movement was, but I think it's safe to say that it has been as impactful on the way people eat all around the world as *nouvelle cuisine* was in the 1970s. Perhaps even more so. →

Before New Nordic, there was the French school where luxury, decadence and high taste triumphed over the frugal efficiency of peasant cooking. The Spanish movement embraced technology in almost impressionistic absurdity. Environmentalism, economics and even health took a back seat to the raw love of gastronomy.

New Nordic dared to question all of that, and to perhaps question globalism itself. Almost bizarrely led by Noma, an extreme, high-end fine-dining restaurant in Copenhagen, New Nordic encompassed ideas of local eating, social justice, environmental impact, health and history.

To truly understand the impact Nordic and Scandinavian food was having on the world stage, it was necessary for us to explore it from every angle – historical, political, environmental and yes, of course, gastronomical.

What we found was a living expression of everything that makes a cuisine great. Not just a single chef pushing the boundaries, or a breakout restaurant daring to be different, but an entire society whose thinking was changing and expressing itself in the most common way any society can – the daily preparation of a good meal to share with those around you.

Pages 96–7: Reindeer, Målselv, Norway
Top left: Making knives the Viking way with Mikkel Helstrom, Bork Havn, Denmark
Top right: A break from reindeer herding, Målselv, Norway
Bottom left: Dried and smoked reindeer fried in butter
Bottom middle: Biking around Copenhagen, Denmark
Bottom right: Hellfried and me, dogsledding in Svalbard

The Danish people recently voted this dish, *stegt flæsk*, their national dish in a country-wide survey. Pork belly is grilled or fried until very crisp, and served with potatoes and a rich white sauce loaded with fresh parsley. It's a bit like a big plate of pork crackling, and for many Danes it is the ultimate childhood memory of comfort food.

FRIED PORK WITH PARSLEY SAUCE

PREPARATION 20 MINUTES
COOKING 45 MINUTES
SERVES 4

1 kg boneless pork belly, cut into slices 1 cm wide

1 tablespoon olive oil

1 kg new potatoes or kipfler potatoes

2 tablespoons salt, plus extra for seasoning

PARSLEY SAUCE

¼ cup (60 g) butter

¼ cup (35 g) plain flour

2 cups (500 ml) chilled milk

½ cup finely shredded curly or flat-leaf parsley, plus extra to garnish

Heat your oven's overhead grill to 200°C. Place the pork on a rack set inside a large roasting tin. Brush the pork with the olive oil and season well with salt on both sides. Cook for 30 minutes, turning halfway through, until the pork is golden and crisp. Remove from the oven and cover loosely with foil. Set aside for 5 minutes to rest.

While the pork is cooking, place the potatoes in a large saucepan and cover with cold water. Add the salt and bring to the boil, then simmer for about 15 minutes, or until the potatoes are tender when tested with a small sharp knife. The knife should enter and exit the potato easily. Drain, then allow to dry in the hot pan with the lid off, to drive out excess moisture.

For the parsley sauce, melt the butter in a saucepan over medium heat. Whisk in the flour and cook for 1 minute. Gradually whisk in the milk, cooking until the sauce has thickened to a thick but pourable consistency, stirring constantly. Season with salt and freshly ground black pepper to taste, then stir the parsley through.

Serve the pork and potatoes with the parsley sauce. Garnish with extra parsley, if desired.

NOTE Every Danish family will have their own preference for this dish. Crispy, golden pork or just browned and juicy. Skin on, or skin off. Pan-fried or oven baked. Just about the only consistent and golden rule for this dish is simple: you can never have too much parsley.

CLAUS MEYER

THERE ARE A FEW ROUTES TO TAKE WHEN TRYING TO DESCRIBE
CLAUS MEYER.

You could try the many labels that are ascribed to him:
chef, professor, author, television presenter, food activist,
restaurateur and entrepreneur, to name a few.

You could try to list his achievements: a television career that
spans more than thirty years, a restaurant empire that turns
over more than $100 million a year, a founder (along with
René Redzepi) of the four-time awarded world's best restaurant
Noma, or the godfather of the New Nordic food movement
that has forever changed the region's cuisine.

I find it best to describe people firsthand. After all, a list of labels
or achievements is just an imprint of a person and not
the person themselves.

I met Claus on a few occasions in Denmark, and I don't
think I've ever met someone who can so magnetically and
compellingly convince a person to their way of thinking.

Claus's philosophy of using food as an instrument to improve
life is an attractive idea, but what is truly extraordinary about
Claus is that he has a talent for taking a grand idea and making
it a grand reality.

The idea of a New Nordic food movement could have stayed just
that – perhaps rolled out in a few speeches, or the subject of a
nice paper sitting in an academic's desk drawer, but in 2003
Claus and René Redzepi took the movement's philosophy
and opened a restaurant called Noma.

In 2004, at a time in their first year when most restaurants are
juggling menus and trying to stay open, the philosophy was
adapted into a manifesto that was subscribed to by Nordic chefs,
food writers and other food professionals. A few years after that,
Claus's idea became a guiding principle for agricultural practice,
industrial food production and government policy across the
region, and the principles of using food as a model for social
change were starting to be emulated from Australia to South
America. To change a cuisine is audacious in itself, but Claus set
his sights on creating a movement, and he achieved just that.

Claus's ambitious idea went on to change the world, so if you
ask me to describe him to you I can only really say one thing:
Claus Meyer is a force of nature.

There is a lovely relationship between many classic Danish dishes. This delicious hen's soup actually doesn't contain any chicken meat at all. A chicken is boiled to make stock, and the meat of the bird is then often used for creamy Chicken and asparagus tartlets (page 107), while the chicken broth is turned into this delicious clear soup, enriched with both pork and dough dumplings.

HEN'S SOUP WITH DOUBLE DUMPLINGS

PREPARATION 40 MINUTES
COOKING 1 ¾ HOURS
SERVES 8

SOUP STOCK

1.5 kg whole chicken

1 celery stalk, finely diced

2 leeks, white part only, halved lengthways, then thinly sliced

3 carrots, cut into 1 cm cubes

1 teaspoon black peppercorns

½ teaspoon salt

bouquet garni of thyme, parsley and bay leaf (optional)

DUMPLINGS

100 g butter

2 cups (300 g) plain flour

1 tablespoon salt

3 eggs

MEATBALLS

300 g minced pork

2 slices white bread, crusts discarded, bread torn

2 tablespoons milk

1 egg

¼ cup (60 g) butter

1 teaspoon salt

½ teaspoon grated nutmeg

Start by making the soup stock. Place the chicken in a large saucepan and add enough water to cover it completely. Bring to the boil over high heat, then drain, discarding the liquid. Rinse the chicken under running water to remove any scum.

Return the chicken to the cleaned saucepan, add enough water to cover the bird again and bring to a gentle simmer. Add the remaining soup stock ingredients, then reduce the heat to low and cook at a bare simmer for 1 hour, skimming off any scum that rises to the surface.

Remove the chicken and discard the bouquet garni, if using. Taste the stock and adjust the seasoning. Reserve the chicken and 1 cup (250 ml) of the stock for the chicken and asparagus tartlets on page 107.

For the dumplings, bring 1 cup (250 ml) water to the boil in a small saucepan. Add the butter and stir until melted, then remove from the heat. Stir in the flour and salt, mixing until smooth, then beat in the eggs one at a time until well combined. Transfer to a bowl and set aside to rest for 20 minutes.

For the meatballs, place all the ingredients in a food processor and pulse until just combined.

Shape the meatball mixture into 2 cm balls, and do the same with the dough mixture. Refrigerate until ready to cook.

To cook the meatballs and dumplings, bring a saucepan of lightly salted water to a simmer. Boil the meatballs (first) and dumplings (second) in batches, just until they float to the surface. Each batch should take just 1–2 minutes of boiling. Remove with a slotted spoon and set aside.

Divide the dumplings and meatballs among soup bowls, then ladle in the hot soup and vegetables.

NOTE This soup, and the companion asparagus tartlets recipe on page 107, are particularly good when made with an older boiling chicken, which has a stronger flavour than the young table birds we're used to eating these days.

I had intended to make this recipe in *Destination Flavour Scandinavia* as a companion to the Hen's soup recipe (page 104), as they are inextricably linked in Danish culinary culture. When making a television program, however, we don't have the luxury of doing everything we want to do, so I was only able to make the soup recipe in the series (asparagus being out of season, among other reasons). I can't tell you how many emails I got from astute viewers asking, 'What happens to the chicken in the soup?!' Thankfully now, in this book, I get to finish the story.

CHICKEN & ASPARAGUS TARTLETS

PREPARATION 30 MINUTES
COOKING 30 MINUTES
MAKES 24 TARTLETS

1 whole cooked chicken
(from page 104)

12 white or green
asparagus spears

3 tablespoons finely
shredded parsley,
to garnish (optional)

TARTLET CASES

6 sheets frozen puff pastry,
thawed

WHITE SAUCE

75 g butter

2 tablespoons plain flour

1 cup (250 ml) Soup stock
(see page 104) or other
chicken stock

1 cup (250 ml) milk

For the tartlet cases, heat your oven to 180°C. Cut four 12 cm rounds from each sheet of puff pastry and place a round into each hole of a standard 12-hole muffin tin. Take an identical muffin tin and stack it on top of the first tin so the pastry is pressed snugly between the two, or use pastry weights. Bake both trays together for 15 minutes, or until the pastry is golden brown and cooked through.

Cool the tartlet cases on a wire rack until they're ready to be filled.

Pick the meat from the chicken, discarding the skin and bones, and cut it into small chunks. Set aside.

Bring a large saucepan of salted water to the boil and blanch the asparagus for about 3 minutes, or until just tender. Chill in iced water, then drain well and cut into 1 cm pieces.

For the white sauce, combine the butter and flour in a small saucepan over medium heat, stirring to create a blonde roux. Add the stock and milk a little at a time, stirring constantly to remove any lumps, and cook the sauce for about 5 minutes, or until it is thick but still pourable. Stir in the chicken meat, asparagus pieces and parsley.

Fill the tartlet cases with the mixture. Grind over a little black pepper, add a sprinkling of parsley if you like and serve immediately.

NOTE If you've planned ahead well enough, instead of blanching the asparagus in boiling water, you can blanch it in the soup stock on page 104 (before cooking the dumplings) and reserve it for the tartlets. It's a small difference, but good cooking is all about taking advantage of every little thing that can make your food taste even a tiny bit better. It all adds up.

In the old Viking harbour of Bork, about two hours from modern-day Copenhagen, Mikkel Helstrom and his friends have built a Viking village by hand, using materials and tools that would have been used in Viking times. While we might think of Vikings as carnivorous pillagers, they actually mainly lived off vegetables and grains, with a bit of seafood thrown in. Their staple meal was a kind of barley risotto flavoured with nettles. This fire-roasted salmon is something that might have been served at a feast to celebrate a glorious victory. The Skagen sauce is a modern touch that works perfectly.

FIRE-ROASTED SALMON
WITH SKAGEN SAUCE & VIKING FLATBREADS

PREPARATION 20 MINUTES
(OR MORE IF YOU'RE CARVING
YOUR OWN PLANKS!)
COOKING 1–1¼ HOURS
SERVES 6

1 × 1.5–2 kg side of
salmon, pin-boned,
skin on

watercress sprigs, to serve

SKAGEN SAUCE

½ cup (125 g) mayonnaise

2 tablespoons sour cream

1 teaspoon dijon mustard

2 tablespoons finely
chopped dill

3 tablespoons salmon roe

finely grated zest of 1 lemon

juice of ½ lemon

VIKING FLATBREADS

2 cups (300 g) plain flour

½ cup (50 g) rye flour

½ cup (75 g) plain or
wholemeal spelt flour

1 teaspoon salt

1½ cups (375 ml) buttermilk

Nail the salmon, flesh side up, to a clean plank of wood with clean wooden nails. Season well with salt.

Place the plank vertically next to a fire, with the fish tail-end up and the plank at a distance where it becomes uncomfortable to hold your hand after 10 seconds. Leave to cook for 20–30 minutes.

Flip the plank vertically so the tail end of the fish is pointing down and leave for a further 20–30 minutes, until the salmon is just cooked through.

To make the Skagen sauce, combine all the ingredients together in a bowl. Taste and adjust the seasoning if required. Set aside.

For the flatbreads, combine the flours and salt in a large bowl, then make a well in the centre. Gradually add the buttermilk, mixing to bring the dough together, then knead for about 5 minutes, until smooth. Roll the dough into 5 cm balls then, using your hands, pinch and flatten the balls out to about 5 mm thick.

Toast the flatbreads in a frying pan or on a hot stone for about 1–2 minutes on each side, until golden in parts and cooked through.

Serve the salmon with the Skagen sauce, flatbreads and watercress.

NOTE We used chestnut wood for the plank, and oak for the wooden nails. To save yourself a little time in the preparation, I highly recommend getting a Viking friend to carve them by hand using Iron Age tools he's forged himself.

DAG LINDEBJERG

THE SEAFOOD SITUATION IN THE NORWEGIAN TOWN OF BERGEN IS UNLIKE ANYTHING I'VE EVER SEEN. AN INTRICATE NETWORK OF SMALL ISLANDS MEANS THAT THE WATERS AROUND THE TOWN ARE A HAVEN FOR HUNDREDS OF DIFFERENT SEAFOOD SPECIES, WHICH COME IN TO ESCAPE THE RAVAGES OF THE NORTH SEA.

Every few weeks a new species swims in and the residents of Bergen, whose summer houses line the shores, either jump in their boats, or just head out to their back decks stretching out over the water and, by pot, net or line, haul in their next meal.

In the summer the waters teem with millions of delicious brown crabs, and a crab pot dropped in the water is sure to be filled when it's next pulled up. It's easier than going to the supermarket.

My guide through the waters of Bergen was Dag Lindebjerg, a man they often call 'Mr West Coast'. What he doesn't know about the waters of Norway's west coast isn't worth knowing.

A former sailor, journalist, broadcaster, sports commentator and Olympic swimming coach, Dag retired in 2013 and spends much of his time aboard his wooden boat *Lindy*, exploring the waterways and fjords of western Norway.

It's an idyllic life, and one I hope one day to emulate. With Dag's long list of accomplishments perhaps he's earned his happiness, but I'll always remember him for teaching me how to make the perfect crab sandwich.

Cooking seafood in the water it was caught in is one of the simplest and most satisfying experiences. It's a perfect representation of connecting yourself to your food, and your food to its surroundings. Sea water doesn't need anything added to it for cooking crustaceans, but a few aromatics can be a great addition if you feel so inclined.

BROWN CRABS IN BEER
WITH BROWN BUTTER MAYONNAISE

PREPARATION 10–15 MINUTES
+ 30 MINUTES CHILLING
COOKING 20 MINUTES
SERVES 4

4 brown crabs or
  2 mud crabs

2 tablespoons salt

2 tablespoons sugar

330 ml bottle of dark lager
  or dark ale

2 lemons, halved

½ bunch dill, roughly torn

lemon wedges, to serve

crusty bread, to serve

BROWN BUTTER MAYONNAISE

200 g butter

100 ml grapeseed oil or
  other neutral-flavoured oil

2 egg yolks

2 tablespoons lemon juice

Chill the crabs for around 30 minutes in the freezer, or on ice, until they are asleep.

Fill a very large pot with clean sea water, or water with salt added. Add the additional salt, sugar, beer, halved lemons and dill and place the pot over high heat.

When the liquid starts to steam, add the crabs and continue to heat. The liquid will start to simmer after 10–15 minutes, at which point it is time to remove the cooked crabs.

For the brown butter mayonnaise, melt the butter in a small saucepan over medium heat and continue to cook for about 5 minutes, until it browns and has a nutty aroma. Add the oil, remove from the heat and set aside for a few minutes to cool slightly.

In a small bowl, mix the egg yolks and lemon juice using a hand-held stick blender, then add the brown butter mixture in a stream until a thick mayonnaise forms.

Serve the crabs immediately, with the mayonnaise, lemon wedges and crusty bread.

NOTE For Dag Lindebjerg's perfect crab sandwich, spread a piece of bread with plenty of the mayonnaise, top with a generous amount of brown crabmeat or tomalley (preferably from a female crab), then add a pile of claw meat (preferably from a male crab) on top. Of course, don't follow this method for crab varieties where catching female crabs is restricted.

This page: Wild boar farming with Peo Andersen in Skåne County, Sweden
Opposite: A coffee break in Copehagen, Denmark

JOHAN & KAREN ANDERS

SPENDING SOME TIME WITH THE ANDERS FAMILY IS ONE OF MY FAVOURITE MEMORIES FROM ALL THE YEARS I'VE BEEN MAKING *DESTINATION FLAVOUR*.

The Anders are Sami reindeer herders, and over two days in the mountains outside the northern Norwegian town of Fossmoen, I herded reindeer with them and had a chance to experience a little of Sami life.

We worked during the day at the tasks of feeding and herding the reindeer, and when the work was done we ate smoked reindeer fried in butter with blood pancakes in the Anders' mountain *gamme*, sometimes known as a *goahti* – a Sami hut made from a timber frame covered and insulated with peat.

While the experience of herding was itself incredible, what really stuck with me about my time with Johan, Karen and their children, Elle and Jon-Ante, was how hard they all worked to preserve their culture.

While reindeer herding might seem anachronistic to modern life, they treat it just as any other farmer would, with modern equipment and technology. They built their mountain gamme by hand but also have an ordinary house in town. It was a privilege to see how a modern Sami family balances their herding traditions with the ordinary business of school pick-ups, homework and regular office jobs.

Sometimes when a history or tradition is so rich, those of us who look from the outside in can let that history overshadow the truth that culture does not exist in a time capsule. It is the practice of culture that keeps it alive, not the memory of it.

I loved this Sami reindeer stew that Karen Anders (see page 117) made for us. The rich, nutty flavour of brown butter in this stew is matched with sweet and spicy raisin bread; while it may seem a little strange, they are a perfect combination.

SAMI REINDEER STEW
WITH BROWN BUTTER & RAISIN BREAD

PREPARATION 30 MINUTES
COOKING 2½ HOURS
SERVES 6

50 g butter

2 kg reindeer chuck,
   cut into 5 cm cubes

2 brown onions, sliced

2 bay leaves

1 cup (250 ml) white wine

8 cups (2 litres) beef stock
   or water

2 teaspoons salt

1 kg potatoes, peeled and
   cut into 3 cm cubes

6 carrots, peeled and cut
   into 2 cm rounds

buttered raisin bread,
   to serve

BROWN BUTTER ROUX

200 g butter

¼ cup (35 g) plain flour

Heat half the butter in a heavy-based saucepan or flameproof casserole dish over high heat. Fry the meat in batches until well browned, then remove from the pan.

Add the remaining butter to the pan and fry the onion for about 5 minutes over medium heat, until lightly browned. Return the meat to the pan and add the bay leaves, wine and stock. Bring to the boil and skim off any scum forming on the surface. Stir in the salt, reduce the heat to a simmer and cook for 2 hours, or until the meat is falling apart.

For the brown butter roux, heat the butter in a separate saucepan over medium heat until golden brown. Add the flour and stir it through until the mixture is thick. Continue to cook and stir the roux for about 10 minutes, until it turns a caramel colour.

Stir the roux through the stew, along with the potatoes. Simmer for 5 minutes, then add the carrots and simmer for a further 15 minutes, or until the vegetables are tender. Grind over lots of black pepper and serve with thick slices of buttered raisin bread.

NOTE If the raisin bread is not your cup of tea, this stew is equally delicious with mashed potato and a dollop of lingonberry jam. Instead of reindeer, you could use venison or even beef chuck.

Salmon from the north of Norway is famous around Scandinavia. Its large size and rich fat make it a real delicacy from the region. This traditional Norwegian style of curing salmon is very simple, and perfect for feeding a crowd. Gravadlax literally means 'buried salmon' and it refers to the salmon being buried under the curing mixture.

GRAVADLAX WITH MUSTARD & DILL SAUCE

PREPARATION 20 MINUTES
CURING 2 DAYS
SERVES 12

1 × 1 kg fillet of salmon (about one whole side), skin on

¼ cup (55 g) sugar

¼ cup (35 g) salt

1 teaspoon freshly ground black pepper

½ cup finely chopped dill

2 tablespoons aquavit or brandy

MUSTARD & DILL SAUCE

3 tablespoons dijon mustard

2 tablespoons sugar

2 tablespoons white wine vinegar

3 tablespoons chopped dill

⅓ cup (80 ml) grapeseed oil

TO SERVE

lemon wedges

1 small red onion, cut into rings

rye crispbreads

lompe (Norwegian potato flatbreads)

Cut across the salmon fillet to divide it into two halves of equal length. Place both halves, skin side down, on a large length of plastic wrap. Mix together the sugar, salt and pepper and scatter the mixture in a thick layer over the exposed flesh of the fish. Scatter the dill over and sprinkle all the flesh with the aquavit.

Sandwich the thinner tail piece on top of the larger one, then wrap tightly with at least two more layers of plastic wrap. Place the fish on a tray and leave to cure in the fridge, flipping it over every 12 hours for the next 48 hours.

When ready to serve, make the mustard and dill sauce. In a small bowl, whisk together the mustard, sugar, vinegar and dill until combined, then slowly whisk in the oil until smooth and emulsified.

To serve, unwrap the fish and place it on a board. Wipe the flesh gently with a wet paper towel to remove the sugar and salt, then wipe it down again with a dry paper towel. With a sharp knife, shave the salmon thinly on an angle, leaving the skin behind.

Serve the salmon with the mustard and dill sauce, lemon wedges, onion rings and slices of crispbread and lompe.

You could also serve the salmon with the Viking flatbreads (page 108).

NOTE If you can't find lompe, you can use potato wraps or even flour tortillas as a substitute.

In Sweden, roast pork with sweet and sour braised red cabbage (rødkål) is a traditional Christmas feast. While caramel potatoes are the norm, I recommend serving this with Double-sided hasselback potatoes (page 124). Add a cured side of salmon (page 120) and you're well on the way to a very impressive Yuletide spread.

CHRISTMAS ROAST PORK LEG WITH CRACKLING & RØDKÅL

PREPARATION 25 MINUTES + AT LEAST 1 HOUR RESTING
COOKING 3¼ HOURS
SERVES 6

3 kg pork leg, bone in

2 tablespoons salt

1 tablespoon caraway seeds (optional)

Double-sided hasselback potatoes (page 124), to serve

RØDKÅL

¼ cup (60 g) butter

1 red cabbage, halved, cut into 1 cm slices

3 tablespoons sugar

½ cup (125 ml) apple-cider vinegar

1 teaspoon salt

3 tablespoons redcurrant jam or cranberry sauce

PAN GRAVY

2 tablespoons plain flour

½ cup (125 ml) white wine

1½ cups (375 ml) strong chicken stock

1 tablespoon apple-cider vinegar

Using a sharp knife, score the skin of the pork all over in thin strips. Place the pork on a rack in the sink and pour boiling water all over the skin. Rub salt all over the skin and flesh. If using the caraway seeds, rub them over the flesh only. Set aside for 1 hour to rest, or refrigerate overnight.

Heat your oven to 240°C, or as high as your oven will go. Place the pork on a rack in a roasting tin. Roast for 30 minutes, then reduce the oven temperature to 180°C and roast for a further 2½ hours (or 25 minutes per 500 g).

While the pork is in the oven, make the rødkål. Melt the butter in a large saucepan over medium heat and cook the cabbage, stirring now and then, for about 5 minutes, or until slightly wilted. Stir in the sugar, vinegar and salt, then cover and simmer for 45 minutes. Stir the redcurrant jam through, add a good grind of black pepper and cook, uncovered, for a further 5 minutes. Set aside and keep warm.

When the pork has finished roasting, remove the pork and the rack from the roasting tin and rest for at least 20 minutes. Spoon most of the rendered pork fat out of the roasting tin, leaving the pan juices behind, then place the roasting tin on the stovetop over medium heat.

For the pan gravy, add the flour to the roasting tin and cook, scraping up any dark residue in the pan, until the flour is well blended with the rendered pork fat and starts to turn a deep brown. Add the wine and stir to create a thick paste. Add the stock a little at a time, stirring to remove any lumps, until a rich gravy forms. Strain the gravy, mix the vinegar through, then adjust the seasoning to taste.

Serve the pork with the rødkål, pan gravy and hasselback potatoes.

NOTE Don't skimp on the gravy. A Swedish roast can be many things, but if it misses the gravy it'll never be a hit.

Created in Stockholm in the 1700s at a restaurant called Hasselbacken, the fancy single-sided accordion-cut potatoes have been a classic for centuries. On the other side of the world, Chinese and Japanese chefs were creating the 'dragon cut' or 'snake cut', a style of cutting long vegetables that created a double-sided concertina-like effect. For the first time ever, we're bringing the two together. Try these and you won't go back to regular hasselbacks again.

DOUBLE-SIDED HASSELBACK POTATOES

PREPARATION 20 MINUTES
COOKING 1 HOUR
SERVES 4

1 kg small potatoes, such as Dutch cream or kipfler, peeled

1 teaspoon salt, plus extra for seasoning

2 teaspoons vinegar

⅓ cup (90 g) butter, melted

150 ml sunflower oil or other mild-flavoured vegetable oil

Place a chopstick on a chopping board. Place a potato right next to the chopstick. Using the chopstick as a stopper, slice the potato, on a 45 degree angle, two-thirds of the way through, in slices 1–2 mm apart.

Now roll the potato over completely, so that the first lot of cuts are face down on the board. Repeat the cuts on the other side, cutting on the same angle, so the cuts on each side are perpendicular to one another, and the potato will not be divided. Cut the remaining potatoes in the same way.

Place the potatoes in a large saucepan and cover with cold water. Add the salt and vinegar and bring to a simmer over medium–high heat. Cook for 15 minutes, then drain gently and allow to air dry for 10 minutes.

Heat your oven to 200°C.

Place the potatoes in a roasting tin. Combine the butter and oil in a bowl, then generously drizzle the mixture over the potatoes and gently toss to coat. Season well with salt.

Roast the potatoes for 45 minutes to 1 hour, gently turning a few times during cooking, until the potatoes are crisp and well browned.

Season with more salt if needed and serve.

NOTES Instead of using a chopstick as a cutting guide, you can place a thin chopping board on top of a larger chopping board, then place the potato along the edge of the smaller chopping board, which will stop your knife cutting all the way through the potato.

Adding salt and vinegar to the boiling water helps the potatoes retain their structure, but you still need to be gentle when handling them so that the delicate cuts you've made don't break apart.

There's no more identifiably Swedish dish than good old Swedish meatballs, and they are still a home-cooked favourite to this day. They're perfect with Pickled cucumbers (page 128) and pickled lingonberries, or lingonberry jam.

SWEDISH MEATBALLS IN CREAM SAUCE

PREPARATION 30 MINUTES
COOKING 25 MINUTES
SERVES 4

¼ cup (60 g) butter

¼ cup (35 g) plain flour

2 cups (500 ml) beef stock

¾ cup (190 ml) pouring cream

Pickled cucumbers (page 128), to serve

pickled lingonberries or lingonberry jam, to serve

MEATBALLS

1½ cups (110 g) loosely packed fresh breadcrumbs

2 tablespoons pouring cream

250 g minced pork

500 g minced beef

1 onion, finely grated

½ teaspoon grated nutmeg

1½ teaspoons salt

¼ teaspoon ground white pepper

MASHED POTATOES

1 kg potatoes

1 tablespoon salt, plus extra for seasoning

200 g butter, chilled and cut into cubes

1 cup (250 ml) milk

Heat your oven to 200°C.

For the mashed potatoes, place the potatoes in a large saucepan, cover with cold water, add the salt and bring to the boil. Reduce the heat to medium and cook for about 15 minutes, or until the potatoes come away easily from a small sharp knife inserted into them. Strain the potatoes and return to the dry saucepan over very low heat for 1 minute to dry. Turn off the heat and allow to steam off for 5 minutes. Mash the potatoes very well, add the butter, then gradually stir in the milk until combined. Season well with sea salt.

For the meatballs, put the breadcrumbs in a large bowl, pour the cream over them and leave to soak for a few minutes. Add the pork, beef, onion, nutmeg, salt and white pepper and mix to combine. Form into small balls and place on a large baking tray. Pour a little water into the base of the tray and bake in the oven for 10–15 minutes, or until the meatballs are just cooked through. Remove from the tray to drain.

Heat a large frying pan over medium heat until very hot, then add half the butter. Cook the meatballs for about 5 minutes, turning until well browned all over; you can do this in batches if you wish. Remove the meatballs from the pan, set aside and keep warm. Do not wash the pan.

To make the sauce, return the pan to medium heat, add the remaining butter and sprinkle the flour over, stirring and scraping any residue from the bottom of the pan. Add the stock a little at a time and bring to a simmer. Cook for 2 minutes, then stir in the cream. Season to taste.

Serve the meatballs drizzled with the cream sauce, with the mashed potato, Pickled cucumber and lingonberries alongside.

NOTE The key to a good Swedish meatball is not the sauce – it's the browned surface the meatballs get when they're fried. Take care of this part and the rest will take care of itself.

These simple pickled cucumbers are a classic accompaniment for Swedish meatballs, but also work well as a sweet-sour foil for salmon, roast chicken and any number of dishes.

PICKLED CUCUMBERS

PREPARATION 20 MINUTES
PICKLING AT LEAST 1 HOUR
MAKES ABOUT 2 CUPS

4 Lebanese cucumbers

1 teaspoon salt

2 tablespoons caster sugar

¼ cup (60 ml) white vinegar

1 tablespoon finely
   shredded parsley or dill

Finely slice the cucumbers into very thin rounds using a mandoline, vegetable peeler or Swedish cheese slicer. Sprinkle the cucumber with the salt and place in a sieve. Allow to drain for 15 minutes, discarding any liquid released from the cucumbers.

In a small bowl, combine the sugar and vinegar with ½ cup (125 ml) cold water, stirring to dissolve the sugar as much as possible.

Add the cucumber and parsley (or dill) and mix gently, then transfer to a press-seal bag or clean jar. Leave to pickle in the fridge for at least 1 hour, or preferably overnight. The pickles will keep for a few weeks in the fridge, but are best used in the first week.

NOTE The more traditional way to remove the liquid from the cucumbers is to place it in layers on a plate with the salt, then weigh the plate down with more plates on top. It's nice to do sometimes, but frankly I think draining the cucumbers in a sieve works just as well.

Pea soup and pancakes is a Thursday institution across Scandinavia, and was originally intended to be a hearty meal leading into a traditional fasting day. Even though fasting is far less common now, the pea soup and pancakes still remain. This version takes the classic dish to a healthier place, focusing on vegetables, using unbleached wholemeal flours, and replacing fresh berries with sweet jams.

THURSDAY PEA SOUP & PANCAKES

PREPARATION 30 MINUTES + OVERNIGHT SOAKING
COOKING 3 HOURS 15 MINUTES
SERVES 8

2 cups (440 g) dried whole yellow peas

2 tablespoons butter

1 onion, finely chopped

1 celery stalk, cut into 1 cm cubes

⅛ cabbage, cut into 1 cm chunks

2¼ cups (200 g) mushrooms, cut into 1 cm chunks

1 carrot, cut into 1 cm cubes

1 bouquet garni

1 teaspoon salt, plus extra for seasoning

sour cream, to serve

mixed berries, to serve

icing sugar, for dusting

RYE & SPELT PANCAKES

½ cup (50 g) rye flour

½ cup (75 g) barley or spelt flour

½ cup (75 g) plain flour

2 tablespoons honey

½ teaspoon salt

4 eggs

2 cups (500 ml) milk

butter, for greasing

Soak the peas in water overnight.

Drain the peas, then add them to a large saucepan, pour in 8 cups (2 litres) water and bring to a simmer over medium–high heat. Cook the peas for about 1 hour, using a whisk to catch and discard the skins as they come away from the peas.

Melt the butter in a large frying pan over medium–high heat. Cook the onion, celery, cabbage, mushrooms and carrot for 6–8 minutes, stirring often, until lightly browned and fragrant. Add the vegetable mixture to the pan of peas, together with the bouquet garni and salt.

Bring to a simmer and cook for 2 hours, or until the peas are tender. Season to taste with more salt.

For the pancakes, combine the flours, honey and salt in a bowl, then stir in the eggs, one at a time. Whisk in the milk to combine. Rest for 20 minutes in the fridge.

Heat a small knob of butter in a large frying pan over medium heat. Pour in ½ cup (125 ml) of the batter and cook for 2 minutes on each side, or until deeply golden and cooked through. Remove from the pan and keep warm while cooking the remaining batter.

Serve the soup with the pancakes on the side, topped with sour cream and mixed berries and dusted with icing sugar.

NOTE Scandinavia is one of the most progressive regions in the world when it comes to food policy. I made this lunch for some very young kids at a school in Malmö, Sweden, that is leading the way in the city's S.M.A.R.T. food program, promoting healthy eating through eating less meat, more vegetables, no junk food and increasing the intake of local and organic produce.

These delicious cardamom-spiced buns are filled with a soft marzipan mixture and plenty of sweetened whipped cream. They're traditionally eaten in Sweden on Shrove Tuesday (or Fat Tuesday, as it's known in Scandinavia), but they've become so popular that now they can be found in bakeries all year round. I still only eat them at the traditional time, though. There's something to be said for giving food its moment.

SWEDISH FAT TUESDAY BUNS

PREPARATION 30 MINUTES +
1 HOUR 45 MINUTES PROVING
COOKING 15 MINUTES
MAKES 12

80 g unsalted butter,
  plus extra for greasing

1 cup (250 ml) milk

25 g fresh yeast or
  12 g dried yeast

40 g caster sugar

3½ cups (525 g) plain
  flour, sifted, plus extra
  for dusting

1 teaspoon salt

2 teaspoons ground
  cardamom

1 teaspoon baking powder

2 eggs, lightly beaten in
  separate bowls

icing sugar, for dusting

FILLING

450 ml thickened cream

2 tablespoons icing sugar

100 g marzipan
  (60% almond), finely
  grated

Melt the butter in a small saucepan over medium heat. Add the milk, then transfer to a large bowl and allow to cool until lukewarm.

Crumble in the yeast and stir until dissolved, then add the caster sugar and stir until dissolved. Stir in half the flour until combined, then add the salt, cardamom, baking powder and 1 lightly beaten egg, stirring to combine.

Gradually add the remaining flour, mixing to a shaggy dough.

Using an electric mixer fitted with a dough hook, knead the dough for 5 minutes, or until smooth and elastic. Place in a lightly greased bowl, cover with a tea towel and leave in a warm place to prove for 1 hour, or until doubled in size.

Punch the dough down. Cut 12 × 80 g portions of the dough with a knife, and roll into balls that are as round as possible. Place them on a large baking tray, at least 5 cm apart. Cover the tray with a tea towel and leave to prove for a further 30–40 minutes.

Heat your oven to 190°C.

Glaze the buns with the remaining beaten egg and bake for 12 minutes, or until the buns are golden and sound hollow when tapped on the base. Transfer to a wire rack to cool completely.

To make the filling, whip 300 ml of the cream and the icing sugar to stiff peaks. Transfer the mixture to a piping bag fitted with a star nozzle.

Cut the top off each bun. Scoop out the centre, tearing it into small pieces into a bowl. Mix the torn bread with the grated marzipan and remaining cream, then divide equally among the holes in the buns.

Pipe the whipped cream over, then replace the bun lids. Dust with icing sugar to serve. These buns are best eaten on the day they're made.

NOTE These are more traditionally made with a strong, high-gluten bread flour, but these days I prefer to use plain flour so they are a little bit more 'cake-y' than 'bread-y'.

I've sometimes seen these called 'Danish doughnut holes' in English, which is actually a bit misleading, as these delicious apple pancakes aren't as sweet as doughnuts. They're meant to be served with jam. It isn't a traditional accompaniment, but I sometimes add a dollop of thick cream too.

DANISH APPLE PANCAKE BALLS

PREPARATION 20 MINUTES +
30 MINUTES RESTING
COOKING 15 MINUTES
MAKES ABOUT 20

2 cups (300 g) plain flour

2 tablespoons caster sugar

1 teaspoon bicarbonate
   of soda

¼ teaspoon salt

4 eggs, separated

2 cups (500 ml) milk

1 vanilla bean, split
   in half lengthways,
   seeds scraped

150 g melted butter,
   plus extra for greasing

icing sugar, to serve

raspberry jam, to serve

FRIED APPLE PIECES

¼ cup (60 g) butter

1 apple, peeled and cut
   into 1 cm chunks

1 teaspoon caster sugar

For the fried apple pieces, melt the butter in a small saucepan over medium heat and fry the apple in the sugar for about 5 minutes, or until softened. Set aside.

In a bowl, mix together the flour, caster sugar, bicarbonate of soda and salt. Whisk the egg yolks in another bowl, adding the milk, vanilla seeds and the melted butter.

Add the wet ingredients to the dry and beat to a smooth batter, then leave to rest in the fridge for 30 minutes.

Whisk the egg whites to stiff peaks, then fold into the batter.

Heat an aebleskiver pan over medium heat and grease with butter. Fill the holes with the batter and push a few pieces of apple into the top of each. Cook for 4 minutes, or until golden, then flip them over in the pan with a toothpick or skewer (it's easier than it sounds). Cook for a further 4 minutes, rolling the pancake balls over to get an even brown crust on the outside.

Remove the pancake balls from the pan, and repeat with the remaining batter. Dust with icing sugar and serve immediately, with jam.

NOTE You'll need a special aebleskiver pan to make these. Alternatively, you could use a Japanese takoyaki pan, or even an electric Dutch pancake maker (which are often just repurposed takoyaki makers from Japan).

We call it a 'Danish', the Danes call it 'Viennese bread' (*Weinerbrød*), but in Vienna they call it 'Copenhagen Plunder' (*Kopenhagener Plunder*), and the most popular variety, the *Spandauer*, is named after a German prison. Confused yet? Well, it doesn't matter because they're absolutely delicious.

This recipe is inspired by the one I had from Danni and Helle Nielsen's bakery, which I visited in Copenhagen.

RASPBERRY & MARZIPAN DANISHES

PREPARATION 1 HOUR + OVERNIGHT CHILLING
RESTING 1 HOUR 20 MINUTES
PROVING 1½–2 HOURS
COOKING 15 MINUTES
MAKES 20

2 eggs, lightly beaten

1⅔ cups (525 g) raspberry jam, or to taste

⅔ cup (70 g) flaked hazelnuts or almonds

1 cup (125 g) icing sugar

DOUGH

400 g cold unsalted butter

2 × 50 g cold eggs

200 ml ice-cold water

30 g fresh yeast, crumbled

3 cups (450 g) plain flour, chilled in the freezer overnight, plus extra for dusting

40 g caster sugar

2 teaspoons salt

MARZIPAN CREAM

100 g caster sugar

100 g marzipan

100 g softened unsalted butter, quartered

For the dough, place the butter between two sheets of baking paper and beat with a rolling pin until it forms a 1.5 cm thick square. Place in the fridge while you make the dough; the butter should be cold but still malleable when rolling with the dough.

Place the remaining dough ingredients in the bowl of an electric mixer fitted with a dough hook. Knead on the lowest speed for no longer than 4 minutes, to ensure you don't overwork the gluten, then transfer to a lightly floured work surface. The dough should feel soft but not sticky; if necessary, add a little extra flour.

Roll the dough out into a 1.5 cm thick square, then place the chilled butter diagonally on top. Using a rolling pin, beat the two opposite corners of the butter to flatten slightly, then bring the two corners of the dough up to meet in the centre. Repeat with the opposite sides, so that the butter is completely encased in the dough; if necessary use your hands to pat down the dough and seal well. It is important there are no holes in the dough.

Making sure your work surface is always lightly dusted with flour, roll the dough out into a 20 cm × 60 cm rectangle. Fold the rectangle from one long end by one-third, then fold the other long end over the top, so you have three layers of butter. Wrap the dough in plastic wrap and refrigerate for 20 minutes, to allow the gluten to relax.

Repeat the rolling, folding and resting process twice more, rotating the dough 90 degrees each time, so that when you roll it out you are stretching it in the opposite direction to the previous fold.

Once the dough has been rolled and folded three times, refrigerate for another 20 minutes to rest further.

To make the marzipan cream, use an electric mixer fitted with a paddle attachment to beat the sugar and marzipan on medium speed for 3–4 minutes, until fully combined. Add the butter, one piece at a time, until just combined; don't overmix. Spoon into a piping bag fitted with a 2 cm nozzle and refrigerate until needed. The mixture will harden if chilled too long; if needed, leave at room temperature until soft enough to pipe.

Line a large baking tray with baking paper. Cut the dough in half. Cover one half and keep in the fridge. On a lightly floured surface, roll out the other half into a 21 cm × 51 cm rectangle, about 5 mm thick. Trim the edges to straighten, then cut into 10 cm squares and place on the baking tray, at well-spaced intervals.

Pipe a little marzipan cream into the centre of each square, then fold the corners into the centre, pressing your thumb into the centre to secure well. Repeat with the remaining dough and marzipan filling.

Cover loosely with a tea towel and stand in a warm, draught-free place for 1½–2 hours, or until almost doubled in size.

Heat your oven to 200°C. Brush the pastries with the beaten eggs. Dip two fingertips of each hand into the egg wash and push into the centre of each pastry, to make a hollow for the jam. Spoon 1 tablespoon jam into each hollow, then scatter with the flaked nuts.

Bake for 10–15 minutes, or until golden and cooked through, then stand on the tray to cool slightly.

To make the icing, combine the icing sugar and 1 tablespoon hot water in a bowl until smooth, then spoon into a piping bag fitted with a very small nozzle. Pipe a ring of icing around the edge of each Danish.

Eat them on the same day you make them.

NOTE Making a yeast-leavened puff pastry and baking your own Danishes isn't the easiest thing in the world, but should you choose to climb that mountain, the view from the top is spectacular enough to make the journey worthwhile.

Raspberry
& marzipan
Danishes
(pages 136–7)

Waffles are a Scandinavian favourite, both at breakfast and as a sweet treat for afternoon tea. In Norway, the waffles are soft, spiked with cardamom and served with a nutty brown goat's cheese, but I love Swedish waffles the best. Made with ice-cold ingredients, they're impossibly crispy.

This is a recipe from a friend's grandmother, who lives in the north of Sweden and uses snow to get the perfect texture. I've adapted it for those of us who aren't living through a Swedish winter.

SWEDISH CRISPY WAFFLES WITH JAM & WHIPPED CREAM

PREPARATION 10 MINUTES
COOKING 15 MINUTES
MAKES ABOUT 10

berry jam, to serve
    (cloudberry and
    blackberry are favourites)

WAFFLES

2 cups (500 ml) ice-cold
    pouring cream

2 cups (300 g) plain flour,
    frozen

2 teaspoons baking powder

1 cup (250 ml) ice-cold
    soda water – or
    2 cups snow

80 g butter, melted

VANILLA CREAM

2 tablespoons icing sugar

½ teaspoon natural
    vanilla extract

300 ml thickened cream

For the waffles, whip the cream to soft peaks in a bowl using an electric mixer. Fold the flour and baking powder through. Just before cooking, stir through the soda water and melted butter.

Place about ¼ cup (60 ml) of batter into a waffle iron and cook until browned and crispy, about 15 minutes.

For the vanilla cream, whip the ingredients together to soft peaks.

Serve the waffles immediately, with the vanilla cream and a good dollop of jam.

NOTE Use a Scandinavian heart-shaped thin waffle iron for best results. If your waffles aren't turning out crisp enough, you might just need to cook them in the waffle iron a little longer.

JAPAN

When we were making *Destination Flavour Japan*, it was our goal to make a series that simply told the truth about the place. It's a country that's fascinated me more than any other, and the challenge was how to present that fascination as succinctly and honestly as possible.

From the outside looking in, Japan can be confusing, and it's easy to supplant confusion with the comforting tunnel vision of cliche. But when you order Japan into nothing more than a series of tropes – robotic salarymen, gaudy Shibuya girls from the 1990s, and stoic artisans in singular devotion to their craft, to name a few – what can often go missing is humanity. →

For me, the humanity of Japan is what makes it beautiful. We told stories of soy sauce makers devastated by the 2010 tsunami. Of retirees following their dreams. Of sushi chefs who connect a person's taste in fish to the vagaries of their personality.

You might ask what all of this has to do with food, but food is the story of humanity. Hidden within a simple meal are clues that unravel the human condition.

Follow the clues in Japanese food, from the rich history of tempura (page 151), to the personal hand-to-hand ritual of sushi (page 158), or the unornamented simplicity of Okinawan taco rice (page 180), and with every bite the true story of Japan emerges.

Pages 142–3: The Seto Inland Sea, Hiroshima
Top left: An afternoon ride on Taketomi Island, Okinawa
Top right: Roadside ramen in Fukuoka
Bottom left: Nyuto Onsen, Akita
Bottom middle: A pickle seller at Nishiki Market, Kyoto
Bottom right: Nabe of pork belly, mountain potato and miso

This simple sea urchin pasta is Hokkaido in a nutshell, combining the taste of the cold-water sea urchin with the famed Hokkaido butter and cream. While those ingredients may not find themselves mixed together in the Italian pasta canon, the best results for this dish will be found by following good pasta cooking technique – from maintaining the texture of the pasta, to the *mantecare* (see page 30).

SEA URCHIN PASTA

PREPARATION 5 MINUTES
COOKING 15 MINUTES
SERVES 2

250 g dried spaghetti

¼ cup (60 g) butter

1 eschalot, very
   finely chopped

2 garlic cloves, very
   finely chopped

2 tablespoons sake

100 ml thickened cream
   or pouring cream

100 g fresh sea urchin

½ teaspoon salt

1 nori sheet, very finely
   shredded, to serve

Bring a large pot of salted water to a rolling boil. Add the pasta and boil until al dente.

Heat a frying pan over medium heat, add the butter, eschalot and garlic and fry for about 2 minutes, or until fragrant and softened but not browned. Stir in the sake and cream and bring to a simmer. Add about one-quarter of the sea urchin, mashing it lightly and combining it with the sauce. Season with the salt.

Drain the pasta, reserving ¼ cup (60 ml) of the cooking water, then add the pasta and reserved cooking water to the frying pan.

Toss the pasta and sauce together vigorously (*mantecare*; see Note on page 30) to create a thick sauce that coats the pasta. Top with the remaining sea urchin and allow the pasta to warm it through.

Scatter with the nori and serve immediately.

NOTE If you don't have nori, this dish is also very good scattered with finely chopped chives.

FUKUKIMI AND MIENA

THE WORLD OF GEISHA IS MORE FASCINATING
THAN I EVER IMAGINED.

I met Fukukimi and Miena in Kyoto, at the Ishihatsu Teahouse,
one of the most famous geisha houses in the Miyagawa area.
They were *maiko*, or apprentice geisha, studying and training
to be elevated to the rank of geisha (or *geiko*, as they're
known in Kyoto).

They spend their days learning the arts, from music and
dance to etiquette and conversation, and theirs is a life
devoted entirely to the pursuit of beauty. It's a bit like rolling
a ballerina together with a concert violinist and opera singer,
along with a world-class poet, all wrapped up into a magnetic
and vivacious hostess.

Of course, Fukukimi and Miena aren't their real names.
Those are stage names, for want of a better word, as geisha are
essentially performers. In many ways, however, the real people
behind the personae are even more intriguing.

Fukukimi decided to become a geisha when she was just a
child. She arrived in Kyoto when she was twelve years old.

What inspires a child of such a young age to choose a geisha's
life? For Fukukimi it was her love of music. She told me how
she first saw geisha as a child when one visited her hometown
in Japan's northern prefectures. The elegant kimono, artful
shamisen playing and flawless makeup were intoxicating to
a young girl from a country town, and she knew then that
this was what she wanted to become.

While their busy schedule of lessons and practice fills most of
every day, on their days off they're just like any other teenage
girls. Messaging friends on their mobiles, or heading to town to
buy a new pair of jeans, catch a movie or meet up with friends.
They even have boyfriends, an idea that might have been
frowned upon a few centuries ago.

In Japan, even the most ancient traditions are evolving, and the
life of a modern day geisha is a twenty-first century life indeed.

Deep-frying originally came to Japan from Portugal around 400 years ago, but since then it has turned into an art form. The secret to a crispy tempura batter is avoiding gluten – a protein in wheat flour that provides strength and elasticity. It's fantastic for breads and noodles but not for crispy batters. Gluten develops through kneading, heat, moisture and time. Freezing the flour in this recipe keeps it dry and cold, inhibiting the formation of gluten – as does mixing the flour with the liquid only at the last minute.

MIXED TEMPURA

PREPARATION 20 MINUTES + OVERNIGHT FREEZING
COOKING 20 MINUTES
SERVES 4 AS PART OF A SHARED MEAL

8 cups (2 litres) rice bran, canola or sunflower oil, for deep-frying

1 Japanese eggplant, sliced diagonally, about 5 mm thick

2 slices pumpkin, about 5 mm thick, seeds removed

2 asparagus spears

2 very large raw prawns

2 boneless whiting fillets, skin and tail on

½ cup (90 g) very finely grated daikon (white radish), excess liquid squeezed out, to serve

TEMPURA BATTER

1 cup (150 g) low-gluten flour or plain flour mixed with 2 tablespoons cornflour, plus extra for dusting

1 egg

1 cup (250 ml) cold water

TENTSUYU (DIPPING SAUCE)

a handful of bonito flakes (katsuobushi)

¼ cup (60 ml) mirin

¼ cup (55 g) caster sugar

¼ cup (60 ml) soy sauce

Sift the flour for the tempura batter onto a tray and chill, uncovered, in the freezer overnight.

For the tentsuyu, bring 2 cups (500 ml) water to the boil in a saucepan and add the bonito flakes. Turn off the heat and stand for 10 minutes, then strain. Return the stock to the pan, add the remaining ingredients and bring to a simmer, stirring to dissolve the sugar. Cool to room temperature.

Heat the oil to 175°C in a wide saucepan or deep-sided frying pan.

For the batter, whisk the egg and water together in a bowl, then add a few ice cubes. Pour half the egg mixture into a separate bowl, sift in half the frozen flour and stir with chopsticks to mix. Don't over-mix – a few lumps are completely fine. (Mix the remaining batter only when you need to.)

Lightly dust the eggplant, pumpkin and asparagus in a little extra flour and draw them through the batter with chopsticks. Lower the vegetables into the hot oil, a few at a time, holding them for a second to stop them sinking to the bottom. Cook for 3–5 minutes, or until they are just tender and the batter is golden, skimming off any bits of batter floating in the oil; save these tempura bits (tenkasu) for making Takoyaki (page 168) or Okonomiyaki (page 170). Drain the vegetables on a wire rack.

To prepare the prawns, remove the shells, keeping the tails intact. Make slits along the undersides of the prawns to stop them curling as they cook.

Increase the oil temperature to 185°C. Repeat the battering and frying process with the prawns and whiting, which should cook in about 3 minutes. Drain on a wire rack.

Serve all the tempura immediately, with a bowl of the tentsuyu, and some grated daikon to mix through it. Any unused tentsuyu will keep in an airtight container in the fridge for about a month.

NOTE Select seasonal ingredients for your tempura. The selection here is a summery mix, but in other seasons choose more appropriate seafood and vegetables. Instead of making the tentsuyu, I often prefer to serve tempura with some good, finely ground salt.

The *nanbanzuke* or 'southern barbarian-style' of marinating was brought to Japan by Portuguese sailors around the sixteenth century, and is reminiscent of the *escabeche* the mariners would have had on their long sea voyages. Those sailors also brought dishes like tempura and castella, a type of sponge cake, which remain popular in Japan to this day.

WHITEBAIT NANBANZUKE

PREPARATION 20 MINUTES + 30 MINUTES SOAKING (OPTIONAL)
COOKING 30 MINUTES + 15 MINUTES RESTING
SERVES 4 AS PART OF A SHARED MEAL

1 small carrot, julienned

1 celery stalk, julienned

½ onion, finely sliced

25 whitebait, about 10 cm in length, or Japanese wakasagi

1 cup (250 ml) milk (optional)

¼ cup (35 g) plain flour

8 cups (2 litres) rice bran, canola or sunflower oil, for deep-frying

½ tsp finely chopped chives, to garnish (optional)

NANBANZUKE DASHI (SEASONED VINEGAR STOCK)

½ cup (125 ml) dashi stock or water

½ cup (125 ml) rice vinegar

2 tablespoons light soy sauce

2 tablespoons mirin

1 dried red chilli, finely sliced

Mix together all the dashi ingredients and transfer to a non-reactive tray, along with the carrot, celery and onion.

If you like, soak the whitebait in the milk for 30 minutes to remove some of the fishy pungency. Drain and pat dry with paper towel, then season with salt and pepper. Dust the fish with the flour to coat.

Heat the oil to 170°C in a wide saucepan or deep-sided frying pan. Deep-fry the fish in batches for 5–6 minutes, or until golden brown and crisp.

Add the whitebait straight from the oil onto the tray of dashi, covering the fried fish with the vegetables. Allow to stand for at least 15 minutes, until the fried coating on the fish takes on a soft and silky texture and the vegetables soften, then transfer to a serving plate. Garnish with chives (if using).

NOTE In Japan this dish is often made with wakasagi, a small oily lake fish. Whitebait (see Note on page 192) or sardines make a great substitute. It's also fantastic with small pieces of fried chicken.

A homemade teriyaki sauce is a revelation for anyone wanting to explore Japanese cuisine. It's dead simple to make, and has only about one-third of the sugar of a commercial sauce. On *Destination Flavour* I made this dish with the flesh from the jawbone of an Ōma tuna from Aomori, the most famous tuna region in the country. Of course, it works perfectly well with any good tuna steak.

TERIYAKI TUNA

PREPARATION 10 MINUTES
COOKING 15 MINUTES
SERVES 4 AS PART OF
A SHARED MEAL

1 large tuna steak, about 300 g

1 teaspoon potato flour or cornflour

1 teaspoon vegetable oil

2 thin spring onions, finely sliced

lemon wedge, to serve

TERIYAKI GLAZE
200 ml mirin

200 ml sake

1 cup (250 ml) soy sauce

¼ cup (55 g) sugar

For the teriyaki glaze, mix all the ingredients together in a small saucepan and stir over medium heat just until the sugar dissolves. Leave to cool, then transfer to a large clean jar or bottle.

With a pastry brush, dust the tuna steak all over with the potato flour.

Heat a frying pan over medium heat until very hot and add the oil. Add the tuna and cook for about 2 minutes on each side, until lightly browned, then remove from the pan.

Add about ¼ cup (60 ml) of the teriyaki glaze to the pan and bring to a simmer. Cook for about 1 minute, or until the glaze is slightly thickened and shiny, then return the tuna to the pan, turning it through the glaze to completely coat the fish.

Transfer the fish to a serving plate and drizzle with the glaze remaining in the pan. Scatter with the spring onion and serve with a lemon wedge.

NOTE Homemade teriyaki glaze is something I always keep in my pantry. This recipe makes about 700 ml, a volume that will fit in an old wine or soy sauce bottle. It keeps in the pantry indefinitely, and it's perfect with salmon, chicken, beef and any number of other dishes. For more ideas on how to use this versatile sauce, subscribe to my YouTube channel at www.youtube.com/adamliaw.

A simple Japanese meal is a study in elegance. A couple of rice balls, a bowl of soup and a few pickles is all you need. Of course, the rice balls can be elaborate, filled with tidbits, flavoured with sprinkles of furikake, or grilled and basted with soy sauce. The soup also can take on any of thousands of different forms, from rich and hearty to delicate and restrained, depending on the ingredients chosen or the type of miso used. Pickles, too, are an entirely separate discipline within Japanese cuisine. With so many millions (billions?) of permutations and possibilities you could be forgiven for falling into confusion, but with Japanese cuisine it's always good to remember that the structure is one of absolute simplicity – and what could be more simple than a ball of rice, a bowl of soup and some pickles?

ONIGIRI, MISO SOUP & PICKLES

PREPARATION 25 MINUTES +
15 MINUTES STANDING
COOKING 25 MINUTES
SERVES 4

2 cups (400 g) koshihikari rice (sometimes called sushi rice)

1 nori sheet, cut into 5 cm × 10 cm rectangles

a selection of Japanese pickles, to serve (see Note)

MISO SOUP WITH CLAMS

5 g piece of dried wakame seaweed

150 g silken tofu, drained

16 small clams, scrubbed

⅔ cup (80 ml) sake

2 tablespoons light-coloured miso paste

2 thin spring onions, finely sliced

Place the rice in a heavy-based saucepan and cover with plenty of water. Use your hand to stir. Pour off the cloudy water and repeat the rinsing process three times. Add more clean water, to reach about 2 cm above the rice. Place uncovered over high heat and bring to a simmer. Continue to simmer for about 5 minutes, until the water level reaches the top of the rice. Cover with a tight-fitting lid and reduce the heat to very low. Continue to cook for 12 minutes, then remove from the heat and stand for a further 5 minutes, without removing the lid. Fluff the rice with the cutting motion of a rice paddle and keep warm until ready to use.

To mould the onigiri, moisten clean hands with water and sprinkle your palms with a little salt. Take a handful of rice and mould it into a triangular puck shape, gently pressing with your palms with a grabbing motion, and rotating the rice in your hands after each grab. Wrap a piece of nori around the rice as pictured.

For the miso soup, soak the wakame in cold water for 5 minutes, until soft. Wrap the tofu in a double layer of paper towel and place a plate on top. Stand for 10 minutes, to squeeze out the excess moisture.

Place the clams, sake and 3 cups (750 ml) water in a small saucepan and bring to a simmer, then simmer for about 2 minutes, or until the clams open. Reduce the heat to very low.

Place the miso paste in a small sieve or large ladle and submerge it just under the surface of the liquid. Using a stirring motion with a spoon, dissolve the miso into the soup. Discard any grit remaining in the sieve or ladle. Keep the heat low to keep the soup warm after adding the miso, but do not let it come back to the boil.

Slice the wakame into 2 cm lengths (if not already sliced) and add to the soup. Cut the tofu into 2 cm cubes and add to the soup.

Stir the spring onion through the soup, then ladle into four small soup bowls. Serve immediately, with the onigiri and pickles.

NOTE Japanese pickles come in hundreds of different shapes, sizes and flavours, and it's very common for Japanese families to make or buy many different varieties to accompany a meal.

The first thing you need to know about making sushi is that Japanese people very rarely (if ever) try to make it at home. Nigiri sushi (the kind of hand-moulded sushi you find at high-end sushi restaurants) is left to the professionals, and *maki-zushi* (sushi rolls) are less popular than they are in the West (and also very rarely made at home).

When Japanese families do eat sushi at home, it will more than likely be *temaki* sushi – hand-rolled sushi. A big bowl of sushi rice (or even ordinary rice) is placed on the table with a selection of fillings, and people just roll their own sushi by hand. It's a bit like family taco night.

HAND-ROLLED SUSHI

PREPARATION 30 MINUTES +
5 MINUTES STANDING
COOKING 20 MINUTES
SERVES 4

½ cup (125 ml) rice wine vinegar

2 tablespoons caster sugar

1 teaspoon salt

4 cups (800 g) koshihikari rice (sometimes called sushi rice)

1 piece of kombu seaweed, about 10 cm square

8 nori sheets, halved or quartered (as you prefer)

a selection of fillings (see Note)

TO SERVE
wasabi

pickled ginger

soy sauce

Combine the vinegar, sugar and salt in a small non-reactive saucepan and place over medium heat, stirring just to dissolve the solids. Remove from the heat and set aside while cooking the rice.

To cook the rice, place it in a heavy-based saucepan and cover with plenty of water. Use your hand to stir. Carefully pour off the cloudy water and repeat the rinsing process about three times, until the water is less cloudy. Add more clean water, to reach about 2 cm above the rice, then add the kombu. Place uncovered over high heat and bring to a simmer, removing the kombu after about 4 minutes, or when it softens enough for a thumbnail imprint to stay in its surface.

Continue to simmer for about 5 minutes, until the water level reaches the top of the rice, and steam holes appear in the surface. Cover with a tight-fitting lid and reduce the heat to very low. Continue to cook for 12 minutes, then remove from the heat and stand for a further 5 minutes, without removing the lid.

After 5 minutes, remove the lid and turn the rice out onto a large tray or wooden basin and fluff the rice with the cutting motion of a rice paddle. Sprinkle the vinegar mixture over a little at a time, fanning the rice to drive off excess moisture and continuing to fluff the rice with the paddle. Continue until the rice has cooled to blood temperature, and enough vinegar mixture has been added to your taste. Cover with a damp tea towel until ready to serve.

Serve the rice with a pile of nori, and your chosen fillings and condiments. To roll the sushi, you just take a square of nori, add a little rice to the centre and flatten it out with your chopsticks. Add the fillings you like and roll it up. A cone shape is a common way to roll it, but you can also roll it like a cigar or even just fold the nori in half like a taco.

NOTE When selecting your fillings, the easiest option is to buy a few plates of sliced sashimi and combine it with batons of avocado, cucumber, sprouts, shiso leaves, lettuce leaves and Japanese omelette. Cooked peeled prawns are good also. Pickled ginger is served with sushi as a palate cleanser; don't be tempted to roll it in with the fillings, as it will overpower the other flavours.

Literally 'meat and potatoes', nikujaga is one of Japan's most popular home-cooked dishes. Every family will have its own version of this light, simmered dish of meat, potatoes and a few other ingredients. It's such a common dish, it's even considered a way to flirt in Japan: a single man asking a single woman if she can make nikujaga implies that he is considering what kind of wife and mother she would be. Ironically, this is my mother-in-law's recipe.

NIKUJAGA

PREPARATION 20 MINUTES
COOKING 25 MINUTES
SERVES 4 AS PART OF A
SHARED MEAL

150 g shirataki noodles (also called konnyaku jelly threads; optional)

1 cup (250 ml) dashi or chicken stock

2 tablespoons sake

2 tablespoons mirin

3 tablespoons soy sauce

2 tablespoons sugar

300 g wagyu beef sirloin, thinly sliced (see Notes), then cut into 6 cm lengths

400 g potatoes, peeled and cut into irregular chunks

1 carrot, peeled and cut into irregular chunks

1 onion, cut into 1 cm slices

15 snow peas

If using the shirataki noodles, drain them well and rinse under cold running water. Bring a small saucepan of water to a rolling boil and add the noodles. Boil for 5 minutes, strain and set aside.

Combine the dashi, sake, mirin, soy sauce and sugar in a large saucepan and bring to a simmer. Add the beef and cook through for just a few seconds, until the meat changes colour. Transfer the meat to a bowl, then cover and set aside.

Bring the stock back to the boil and skim off any foamy scum that rises to the surface. Add the potato and carrot and cover with a wooden drop lid (see Notes below) or a cartouche of baking paper (see Note on page 59), or both. Simmer for 10 minutes.

Add the onion and shirataki noodles, if using. Replace the drop lid or cartouche and simmer for a further 10 minutes, until the vegetables are very soft and the liquid is nearly completely gone. Stir the beef through, cover again and allow to cool.

To serve, blanch the snow peas in boiling salted water for 1 minute. Reheat the stew, and gently mix the snow peas through.

NOTES The meat for nikujaga needs to be very thinly sliced. You can buy paper-thin slices of frozen wagyu beef from Asian grocery stores. If your beef is not heavily marbled, you can return it to the pot at the same time as the onions so it cooks a little more and becomes tender.

Drop lids (*otoshibuta*) are used for long simmering in Japanese cooking to hold the ingredients in the simmering liquid, while also allowing some steam to escape so that the liquid reduces, and to stop soft ingredients bouncing around too much and losing their structure.

KIYOE NODA

KIYOE NODA IS FOLLOWING HIS FAMILY TRADITION OF MAKING MISO, AS THE HEAD OF MASUZUKA MISO, BUT IT HASN'T ALWAYS BEEN THAT WAY.

As a young man Kiyoe was a baseball prodigy, destined for the big leagues. Tragically, a shoulder injury ended his baseball dreams. Returning to the family business, he found another dream – one that he says is the most important part of life.

You see, food is a gateway to culture and philosophy. The process of making miso is simple enough, but Noda-san says it all needs to be connected to nature.

His miso is made the natural way, fermented and aged in giant vats made of Japanese cypress and weighted down with rocks from the centre of a fast-flowing river. The water knocks away the weaker parts of the rock, leaving only the smoothest and densest stones. He plays music to the miso – lullabies to help it sleep – and as it ages through the four seasons of the year, the fluctuations in temperature and humidity give the miso a tempo and a heartbeat.

Noda-san has even built a school within the walls of his factory, right among the barrels. Every week he teaches local children about miso, and about their history and culture.

'Teach the children first,' he says, 'and then the children can teach their parents'.

I love the visual contrast between the light and dark dengaku miso sauces in this simple eggplant dish.

These sweet dengaku miso sauces are a perfect match with eggplant, but also work well with grilled tofu, rice cakes, simmered daikon and even potato. This recipe makes more than you need, but the leftover dengaku sauces will keep in the fridge indefinitely, for whenever you need them.

Thin Japanese eggplants are traditional, but to be honest I prefer this dish with the fatter, bulbous European eggplants.

EGGPLANT WITH DENGAKU MISO

PREPARATION 10 MINUTES
COOKING 1 HOUR
SERVES 4 AS PART OF
A SHARED MEAL

1 European eggplant or
3 Japanese eggplants,
halved lengthways

1 tablespoon rice bran oil
or other vegetable oil

toasted white and black
sesame seeds, to serve

1 tablespoon finely chopped
chives, to serve

**LIGHT DENGAKU MISO
(MAKES EXTRA)**

100 g white miso (or other
light-coloured miso)

2 tablespoons sake

2 tablespoons mirin

2 tablespoons sugar

**DARK DENGAKU MISO
(MAKES EXTRA)**

100 g hatcho miso
(red miso)

2 tablespoons sake

2 tablespoons mirin

2 tablespoons sugar

Heat your oven to 180°C.

Using a sharp knife, trim a little off the 'cheek' of each eggplant half, to make a flat base so it sits level on the baking tray. Score a cross-hatch pattern in the open face of the eggplant. Drizzle with the oil and bake for 45 minutes to 1 hour, until the eggplants are tender but still holding their shape.

For the light dengaku miso, mix the ingredients in a small saucepan with 2 tablespoons water and bring to a simmer. Simmer for a few minutes, stirring regularly until the mixture thickens to a very thick, but still pourable, consistency. Transfer to a bowl and set aside.

Rinse the pan and repeat the process for the dark dengaku miso.

When the eggplant is cooked, generously top one eggplant half with the light dengaki miso, and the other with the dark dengaku miso.

Switch the oven to a hot grill setting. Return the eggplant to the oven and grill for about 5 minutes, or until the miso is bubbling.

Transfer the eggplant to a serving plate. Scatter the light dengaku miso with black sesame seeds, and the dark dengaku miso with white sesame seeds. Sprinkle all the eggplant with chopped chives and serve.

NOTE The colour of miso paste is often a good guide to its flavour. A dark miso is made with a higher proportion of soy beans, and will be strong and savoury, while a paler miso will have higher proportions of other grains like barley or rice, and have a milder flavour.

Kara-age is one of my favourite Japanese dishes and can be found on izakaya menus everywhere. An izakaya is a casual style of Japanese restaurant found all over Japan, and they're a great place to catch up with friends to share a good meal and a few cold beers. *Kara-age* means 'empty fry' or 'naked fry', which refers to the chicken being fried without a thick batter; instead, a flavourful soy-based marinade sits underneath a very light flour coating, giving the dish its name.

Frying the chicken in three short blasts at high heat with rests in between produces a crispy outer coating, while residual heat gently cooks the interior, for tender and succulent meat.

TRIPLE-FRIED KARA-AGE

PREPARATION 15 MINUTES + 15 MINUTES STANDING
COOKING 15 MINUTES
SERVES 4 AS PART OF A SHARED MEAL

3–4 boneless chicken thighs (about 600 g), skin on

¼ cup (60 ml) light soy sauce

2 tablespoons sake

1 tablespoon grated fresh ginger, juice only

½ teaspoon sugar

¾ cup (90 g) potato flour or cornflour

8 cups (2 litres) rice bran, canola, sunflower or other vegetable oil, for deep-frying

TO SERVE
lemon slices

Japanese mayonnaise

shichimi togarashi (Japanese seven-spice, optional)

Cut the chicken into 5 cm pieces. Combine in a bowl with the soy sauce, sake, ginger juice and sugar and stand for 10 minutes.

Place the flour on a tray or in a large bowl. Using chopsticks, pull the chicken out of the marinade and drop it into the flour, one piece at a time. (Adding the pieces one at a time helps avoid pouring in too much marinade, and stops the chicken sticking together.) Shake any excess flour from the chicken and place on a tray in a single layer.

Allow the floured chicken to stand, uncovered, for at least 5 minutes before frying.

In a wide saucepan, heat the oil to 180°C.

Working in batches, deep-fry the chicken three times. For each batch, deep-fry the chicken for 1 minute, then transfer to a wire rack and rest for 30 seconds. Return the chicken to the oil and fry for 30 seconds, then rest on a rack again for another 30 seconds. Add the chicken back into the oil for one last blast of 30 seconds to 1 minute, then rest for 2 minutes on a rack.

Serve the chicken with lemon slices and Japanese mayonnaise; add a sprinkling of shichimi togarashi if desired.

NOTE Allowing the coated chicken to stand for 5 minutes before frying allows the flour to absorb the flavour of the marinade, and then dry slightly. This little resting time is the secret to producing crispy and flavourful kara-age.

A takoyaki party is a brilliant way to entertain at home, particularly with kids. Gather around the takoyaki pan and cook your own, varying the fillings as you wish. I've made takoyaki filled with crab, prawn, cheeseburger ingredients, and with squid ink batter – the possibilities boggle the mind.

We always finish our takoyaki parties with a round of Danish apple pancake balls (page 135), too.

TAKOYAKI

PREPARATION 30 MINUTES
COOKING 45 MINUTES +
ABOUT 10 MINUTES PER BATCH
MAKES ABOUT 50

1 medium-sized octopus, about 800 g; this will leave extra octopus for other purposes

¼ cup (60 ml) vegetable oil, for greasing the pan

TAKOYAKI BATTER

1⅔ cups (250 g) plain flour

4 cups (1 litre) bonito stock, other stock or water

2 eggs, beaten

½ teaspoon soy sauce

¼ teaspoon salt

FILLINGS AND TOPPINGS

1 cup tenkasu (tempura batter bits; see page 151)

3 tablespoons finely chopped red pickled ginger (benishouga)

½ cup (30 g) finely sliced spring onions

1 cup (250 ml) Otafuku sauce

1 cup (250 ml) Japanese mayonnaise

2 tablespoons aonori (dried bright green laver seaweed flakes)

a handful of bonito flakes (katsuobushi)

Remove the hood and beak of the octopus, so just the tentacles remain.

Bring a large pot of salted water to a simmer, then slowly lower the octopus into the water – the legs should curl as the octopus is being lowered in. Leave to simmer for 30–45 minutes. The amount of time you need to cook the octopus will depend on its size. A smaller octopus simmered for 45 minutes may be too tender so, if in doubt, err on the side of caution and cook the octopus for a shorter amount of time. For this dish is it better for it to be slightly firm, rather than too soft.

Remove the octopus from the pot and cut it into 1.5 cm cubes, reserving all but about 50 cubes for another purpose.

To make the batter, combine all the ingredients with a whisk and whisk to a very thin, watery batter.

Arrange all the fillings and toppings on the table.

Heat a takoyaki pan (or aebleskiver pan, see pages 134–135) until it is hot. Brush with oil, then ladle in the batter, completely filling the holes in the pan, as well as the surrounds. Drop an octopus cube into each hole, then scatter the entire pan with tenkasu, pickled ginger and spring onion. As the batter starts to firm, draw lines between the holes with a skewer, as if marking out a grid. Insert the skewer to the base of each hole and roll the ball over to create a sphere. Cook for a further 5 minutes or so, rolling the balls over periodically until they are crisp on the outside.

Remove the balls from the pan and arrange on a plate. Repeat with the remaining batter.

To serve, drizzle the takoyaki liberally with okonomiyaki sauce and mayonnaise, and scatter with the aonori and bonito flakes.

NOTE Bonito flakes, benishouga, tenkasu, Otafuku sauce, Japanese mayonnaise and aonori are all readily available at Asian and Japanese grocers. If you can't find a few of them, just improvise. You can use chicken stock instead of bonito stock, pink or yellow pickled ginger instead of benishouga, puffed rice instead of tenkasu (or just leave them out), chopped chives instead of aonori, and make your own okonomiyaki sauce by mixing some tomato sauce and worcestershire sauce with a bit of mustard.

As close cousins, takoyaki and okonomiyaki are two of the most loved Osakan dishes, both in Osaka and around Japan. They use many of the same ingredients, and can be adapted to create new flavour combinations. This recipe plays with my favourite combination of fillings – pork, prawn and grated cheese – but you can use just about anything. Experiment!

OKONOMIYAKI (OSAKA-STYLE)

PREPARATION 20 MINUTES +
30 MINUTES STANDING
COOKING 1 HOUR
SERVES 4

½ head of cabbage (about 500 g), finely chopped

200 g pork belly, skin removed, cut into 1 cm pieces

1 cup roughly chopped raw prawn meat (about 200 g)

½ cup tenkasu (tempura batter bits; see page 151)

2 tablespoons red pickled ginger (benishouga)

½ cup (60 g) grated cheese

1 cup (250 ml) Otafuku sauce, to serve

½ cup (125 ml) Japanese mayonnaise, to serve

2 tablespoons aonori (dried bright green laver seaweed flakes), to serve

bonito flakes (katsuobushi), to serve

OKONOMIYAKI BATTER

2 cups (300 g) plain flour

½ cup (60 g) potato flour or cornflour

1½ cups (375 ml) bonito stock, other stock or water

2 eggs

For the batter, mix all the ingredients together in a large bowl and leave to stand in the fridge for 30 minutes before using.

In a large bowl, mix together the cabbage, pork, prawn meat, tenkasu and pickled ginger, pour the batter over and mix well. (Alternatively, you can make a few different flavours of okonomiyaki by dividing the cabbage, tenkasu, benishouga and batter mixture equally among four bowls, and mixing different fillings into each bowl separately.)

Lightly oil a hot teppanyaki plate or large frying pan. Scoop one-eighth of the okonomiyaki mixture onto the hotplate or pan and gently spread out to a circle, about 15–20 cm in diameter. Sprinkle with one-eighth of the cheese, then top with another one-eighth of the mixture – but do not press the mixture down.

Cook over medium–low heat for about 10 minutes, until the bottom is browned, moulding the cake around the edges to create a circle.

Flip the okonomiyaki over, press it down firmly and poke a few holes in the top to allow steam to escape. Cook for a further 5 minutes, until the thick pancake is cooked through, then transfer to a serving plate.

Repeat the process three times, to create four okonomiyaki. (I will often cook one okonomiyaki at a time in each of two separate frying pans, and then repeat that process.)

To serve, brush each pancake liberally with Otafuku sauce, drizzle with lots of mayonnaise and scatter with aonori and bonito flakes.

NOTE To create an attractive pattern with the mayonnaise, cover the okonomiyaki with Otafuku sauce first, then squeeze the mayonnaise from the bottle in parallel lines about 2 cm apart. Draw a chopstick across the top of the Otafuku sauce in long strokes 2 cm apart, perpendicular to the lines of mayonnaise.

TAKAHIRO INOUE

I MET INOUE-SAN ENTIRELY BY CHANCE. WE WERE AT THE YAMATO RAMEN SCHOOL IN TOKYO TO FILM WITH THE PATRON OF THE SCHOOL, KAORU FUJII.

I wanted to learn more about Fujii-san's approach to making ramen. He calls his approach 'digital cooking' and it multiplies cookery, art, science, humour and philosophy to create a unique and reproducible bowl of ramen for every one of his students at the school.

Inoue-san was one of the students at the school. As soon as we met him our director, Scott Thomson, knew Inoue-san had a story to tell. Scott doesn't speak Japanese, but he has a nose for these things.

Inoue-san had worked in insurance for more than thirty years, and after he retired in his sixties, his wife passed away from an illness. He says that tragedy changed his outlook on life.

He decided to do the things he'd always wanted to do, before it was too late, and his dream was to open his own ramen shop in China. Attending the ramen school was his first step.

For a guy who spent a career in insurance, who told me with tears in his eyes he'd never taken a risk in his whole life, his ambition took my breath away. As I was interviewing him I excused myself and left the room. I was getting emotional and I didn't want him to see me cry.

For all the art and science of cooking, Inoue-san showed me that the most important reason behind it all is *why* we cook, and who we do it for.

Inoue-san's ramen store opened in Hangzhou, China, in 2013, and is a thriving success today. As he said to me all those years ago …

'Dreams are better when they're big.'

Ramen is truly not a dish that lends itself to being made at home. The stocks can be incredibly complex and cooked for hours and hours. The *chashu* (the Japanese term for the braised rolled pork that is a traditional topping for ramen) needs to be made at least a day in advance, and the noodles need to be cooked just one serve at a time. A good ramen would have to be one of the most complex dishes in the world, and is certainly best left to the professionals.

That said, tantan ramen has a relatively simple soup base and a short cooking time, so whenever I make ramen at home, this is the one I go for.

TANTAN RAMEN

PREPARATION 1 HOUR +
4 HOURS STEEPING
COOKING 1 HOUR
SERVES 6

3 bok choy or pak choy, quartered lengthways

400 g thin ramen noodles

4 spring onions, finely sliced, to serve

1 tablespoon chilli oil, to serve

SIMPLE SOY-STEEPED EGGS

6 eggs

2 cups (500 ml) bonito stock or chicken stock

¼ cup (60 ml) soy sauce

SOUP BASE

6 garlic cloves, peeled

1 small onion, peeled

5 cm piece of fresh ginger, peeled

¼ cup (60 ml) rice bran oil or other vegetable oil

1 teaspoon sichuan peppercorns, ground

2 tablespoons mild Korean chilli powder

¾ cup (200 g) tahini

12 cups (3 litres) bonito stock or chicken stock

2 tablespoons sesame oil

¼ cup (60 ml) soy sauce

For the soy-steeped eggs, prick the base of each egg shell with a needle to allow air to escape. Bring a pot of water to a rolling boil and lower the eggs in. Start a timer for 6½ minutes. Stir the eggs for the first minute, then do not stir again. When the timer goes, transfer the eggs to a basin of iced water to cool. When cool, peel the eggs and transfer to a small jug with the bonito stock and soy sauce, so that the eggs are completely submerged. Refrigerate for at least 4 hours, gently stirring once or twice.

To make the soup base, place the garlic cloves, onion and ginger in a small food processor and blend to a smooth purée. Heat a large heavy-based saucepan over medium heat and add the oil. Fry the purée for about 10 minutes, or until very fragrant, stirring constantly. Add the sichuan pepper and chilli powder, stirring until fragrant. Stir in the tahini, stock and remaining ingredients, then simmer for 20 minutes, until well combined. Taste and adjust the seasoning. If the soup tastes too bitter from the tahini, add a little more vinegar and sugar. With a stick blender, blend the soup until it is smooth and creamy.

For the pork topping, heat a frying pan over medium–high heat and add the oil. Fry the spring onion and garlic for a few minutes until fragrant, then add the pork and fry, stirring occasionally, until well browned. Add the tobanjian and sesame seeds and toss until fragrant and combined, adding a little water or extra oil to moisten the mixture if necessary.

Bring a large pot of water to the boil and blanch the bok choy for about 3 minutes, until tender. Set the bok choy aside and keep the water boiling to cook the noodles.

Boil the noodles in individual portions until just al dente. The timing for cooking your noodles will vary depending on the particular brand or type of noodles you are using.

2 tablespoons mirin

2 tablespoons sake

1 teaspoon salt

2 teaspoons sugar

¼ cup (60 ml) rice vinegar

PORK TOPPING

¼ cup (60 ml) vegetable oil

3 spring onions, finely sliced

2 garlic cloves, roughly chopped

300 g minced pork

2 tablespoons tobanjian (Sichuan-style chilli bean paste)

1 teaspoon toasted sesame seeds

Time is of the essence here so, even when making multiple bowls, it's best to assemble the ramen just one or (at maximum) two bowls at a time. If the noodles sit in the hot soup for too long (even just a few minutes) they will start to 'stretch', completely ruining the dish.

Working quickly, transfer the noodles to a bowl.

For each serving, top with the stock, a few pieces of bok choy and 2 tablespoons of the pork topping, including a little of its oil. Add a soy-steeped egg (halved, if you prefer), scatter with spring onion, drizzle with a little chilli oil and serve immediately.

NOTE Ramen is not a dish to be lingered over. I usually order my ramen noodles as firm as possible (*katame*, in Japanese) so they don't become too soggy. They say a bowl of ramen should be finished within 7 minutes of making, as soggy, stretched noodles are the enemy of good ramen. You don't want to go to all the effort of making a delicious soup base just to have it ruined by flabby noodles.

This page: Kakigori in Tokyo; a shaved ice sweet served this time with green tea syrup, sweet red beans and mochi
Opposite: Tantan ramen (page 174)

Originally adapted from Chinese jiaozi dumplings, gyoza have become one of Japan's favourite foods. In fact, *jiaozi*, *gyoza* and *gow gee* are the Mandarin, Japanese and Cantonese pronunciations of the exact same word. The main difference between the Japanese version and its Chinese predecessors is that where the Chinese favour a juicy, springy filling, the emphasis of the Japanese dish is on a fine, crispy skin. To save time, you could use commercial dumpling wrappers instead of making your own.

GYOZA

PREPARATION ABOUT 2 HOURS, DEPENDING ON HOW FAST YOU CAN FOLD ALL THE GYOZA
COOKING 15 MINUTES PER BATCH
MAKES ABOUT 50

250 g Chinese cabbage

1 teaspoon salt

500 g fatty minced pork

6 spring onions, very finely chopped

2 garlic cloves, very finely chopped

1 teaspoon grated fresh ginger

2 tablespoons soy sauce, plus extra to serve

1 tablespoon sake

a good pinch of sugar

1 teaspoon vegetable oil, for brushing

1 tablespoon potato flour or cornflour

1 teaspoon sesame oil

rice vinegar, to serve

chilli oil, to serve

HOT WATER GYOZA SKINS

2 cups (300 g) plain flour

1 cup (250 ml) boiling water

For the gyoza skins, put the flour in a bowl, add the boiling water and mix well. Knead for about 5 minutes, dusting with just a little more flour as necessary, until the dough is smooth and firm. Cover with plastic wrap and rest for 30 minutes.

To make the filling, finely shred the cabbage and mix with the salt. Transfer to a strainer and leave to strain for 15 minutes. Squeeze out any excess moisture and mix the salted cabbage in a bowl with the pork, spring onion, garlic, ginger, soy sauce and sake.

On a floured board, roll the dough into a long sausage about 2 cm in diameter. Cut into 1 cm rounds. Press each one down with your palm, then use a small rolling pin to roll into thin round skins, about 7 cm in diameter. Spread about a teaspoon of filling into the centre of a gyoza skin and fold it in half, crimping the edge. Repeat with the remaining filling and skins. (You can now freeze the gyoza if making them ahead.)

Heat a frying pan over medium heat and brush with oil. Place about half the gyoza into the pan, nestling them together to fill the base of the pan, with the gyoza just touching. Fry for about 1 minute, until lightly browned on the bottom.

Mix 2 teaspoons of the potato flour or cornflour into 1 cup (250 ml) water, to make a slurry, and pour it around the gyoza. Cover the pan, with the lid open just a crack, and steam for 7 minutes. Uncover the pan until the water is fully evaporated, and you can hear the gyoza frying instead of boiling. Sprinkle with a little sesame oil and cook for a further minute, then remove the pan from the heat. (This cooking method will produce a 'skirt' of crispy batter between each gyoza that holds them together, but if you don't want the theatre of making the 'skirt', you can just fry-steam the gyoza, using plain water instead of the flour slurry.)

Invert a serving plate over the pan, then flip the pan and plate over, so the gyoza are on the plate. Repeat for the remaining gyoza.

Serve with extra soy sauce, rice vinegar and chilli oil for dipping.

The history of taco rice is one of practical simplicity. After the Second World War, the islands of Okinawa became host to a number of US military bases, many of which remain today. Taco rice dates to just 1984, when it originated in an eatery called Parlor Senri, opened by Matsuzo Gibo in Kin Town just outside the Camp Hansen military base.

Surplus rations of taco seasoning were sold into the communities surrounding the base and, instead of the taco shells and tortillas used in American-style tacos, Gibo used rice – and 'taco rice' was born. The dish soon became a huge hit with locals and US service personnel alike.

On *Destination Flavour* I cooked my fancy-pants version of this very simple dish, but I thought in this book I'd go straight to the heart of it – with packet taco seasoning and bottled salsa, just like it's made in Okinawa. This version is as close as it comes to a piece of history, and is still what's served at my favourite taco rice place, King Tacos, which Gibo opened as a permanent home for his now-iconic dish.

TACO RICE

PREPARATION 10 MINUTES
COOKING 20 MINUTES
SERVES 4

2 tablespoons vegetable oil

500 g minced beef

1 packet of taco seasoning, suitable for 500 g beef

1 tablespoon soy sauce

150 ml bonito stock, chicken stock or water

8 cups (1.5 kg) warm, cooked short-grain rice

6 cups (200 g) finely shredded iceberg lettuce

2 ripe tomatoes, halved and sliced

4 cups (500 g) shredded cheese; tasty, cheddar or American-style cheese work well

1 cup (250 g) mild salsa, to serve

Heat a frying pan over medium heat and add the oil, and then the beef. Fry for a few minutes, stirring occasionally, until well browned, then add the taco seasoning, soy sauce and stock. Bring to a simmer and gently cook, stirring occasionally, for about 10 minutes, or until the stock has evaporated and the meat is flavourful.

For each serve, place a mound of warm rice on a large oval plate and top with one-quarter of the beef mixture. Top with lettuce, lay a few slices of tomato on top and scatter with cheese. Serve with the salsa.

NOTE King Tacos doesn't serve it, but one of my favourite accompaniments with taco rice is koregusu, an Okinawan condiment similar to chilli vodka. Hot bird's eye chillies are soaked in Okinawa's local liquor, awamori, for years, and a few splashes of it really lifts the dish. I've had some chillies soaking in awamori for 10 years now, and the flavour just keeps developing, as it does for any aged alcohol.

A *donburi* is a Japanese rice bowl, and is also the term given to a dish of ingredients served over rice in such a bowl. The oyakodon is perhaps Japan's most famous donburi, and its name translates as 'parent and child', a tongue-in-cheek reference to the fact that it serves both the meat of a chicken and its eggs. Although the chicken is usually cooked by just simmering in its sweet sauce, this version grills the meat for extra depth of flavour.

You could also omit the soy sauce, sake, mirin and sugar and instead use about ½ cup (125 ml) Teriyaki glaze (see page 154). That's what I usually do.

OYAKODON

PREPARATION 20 MINUTES
COOKING 20 MINUTES
SERVES 4

1 tablespoon vegetable oil

4 boneless free-range chicken thighs, skin on (preferably)

2 cups (500 ml) bonito stock or chicken stock

¼ cup (60 ml) soy sauce

2 tablespoons sake

2 tablespoons mirin

2 tablespoons sugar

2 brown onions, cut into 1 cm slices

8 extra-large free-range eggs, beaten

TO SERVE

8 cups (1.5 kg) warm, cooked short-grain rice

4 thin spring onions, finely sliced

1 nori sheet, cut into 5 cm strips, then very finely sliced

shichimi togarashi (Japanese seven-spice), for sprinkling

Heat a large frying pan over medium heat, add the oil and fry the chicken for about 3 minutes, or until well browned all over, particularly on the skin; the chicken should not be cooked through. Remove from the pan and cut into 5 cm pieces.

Add the stock, soy sauce, sake, mirin and sugar to the pan. Stir in the onion and bring to a simmer. Return the chicken to the pan and simmer for about 2 minutes, then reduce the heat to low and pour in the beaten egg. Stir with just a few strokes of a wooden spoon, then continue cooking for about 2 minutes, until the egg begins to set.

To serve, divide the rice among four bowls, then slide one-quarter of the chicken and egg mixture on top of each bowl. Top with a scattering of spring onion, some shreds of nori and a sprinkling of shichimi togarashi.

NOTE In Japan there are specfic oyakodon pans that set the egg just to the size of a rice bowl. They have vertical handles, and when they're removed from the heat the bottom of the pan is pressed onto a wet towel to draw the heat away and prevent the egg overcooking.

Yatai, open-air roadside eateries, line the streets in Fukuoka

These dense, cakey fried doughnuts (*sata andagi*) are a great way to showcase the complex molasses flavours of Okinawa's famed black sugar. Their signature cracks are said to resemble the happy smiles of the Okinawan people. These doughnuts are great with a morning cup of coffee.

OKINAWAN BLACK SUGAR DOUGHNUTS

PREPARATION 20 MINUTES +
30 MINUTES RESTING
COOKING 50 MINUTES
MAKES ABOUT 25

3 extra-large free-range
    eggs

1 cup (180 g) okinawan
    black sugar or dark
    brown sugar

1 tablespoon melted butter

2⅓ cups (335 g) plain flour

2 teaspoons baking powder

8 cups (2 litres) vegetable
    oil, for deep-frying, plus
    extra for oiling

Cream the eggs and sugar together, using a whisk or electric mixer, then whisk the melted butter through. Sieve the flour and baking powder into the mixture, then fold through with a spatula. Chill in the fridge for 30 minutes.

Heat the oil to 150°C in a wide saucepan or deep-sided frying pan.

Rub your hands with a little oil, take some batter and form into a golf ball–sized ball. For each batch, gently drop about six balls into the oil and slowly fry for about 10 minutes, until deep golden brown. You do not need to touch the balls as they will flip themselves over twice in the oil. The first flip comes when the base of the doughnuts expands in the hot oil, and the second flip comes when the cracks form in the dough.

Remove the doughnuts from the oil and drain on a wire rack. I like to eat these fresh and warm, but in Okinawa they are often served at room temperature, sometimes hours after being made.

NOTE If your doughnuts don't form the required cracks, it may be that your oil is too hot, or that your dough is too wet or too dry.

NEW ZEALAND

New Zealand is one of those captivating places that stays with you.

It gets its hooks in, but not in the way destinations like Tokyo, Paris or New York might, with their whirlwinds of hustle and bustle that challenge you to lose yourself in their energy. For New Zealand, the feeling is less like being lost, and more like being found.

Once you've spent even a bit of time in the country, the easy pace of life, the unimaginable natural beauty and, of course, yes, the remarkable food feel unmistakably familiar. Every person you meet feels like a friend, and every place you go feels like home. →

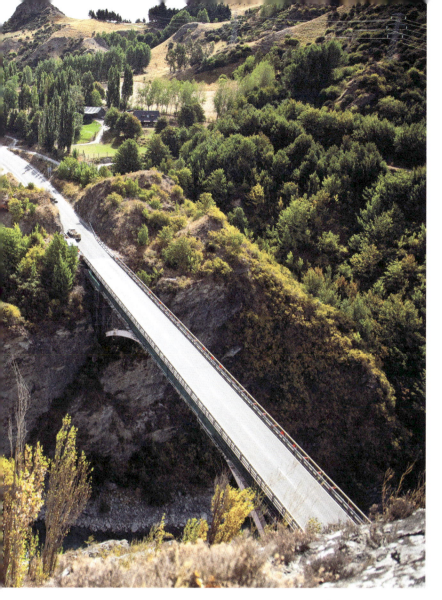

There's a comforting history to the food of New Zealand that makes it all seem very personal. Every dish has a story to tell. The first trout (which were brought over from Scotland alive and packed in wet moss, to stock the New Zealand streams that now teem with them). The kumara (which came centuries before on the boats of the Maori, who came to settle here a long way from the Pacific islands they navigated from). It's this self-assurance with its food history that makes New Zealand seem very comfortable with its culinary identity, and with good reason. They know what they like, and they know they do it well.

The cross-Tasman war between Australia and New Zealand over who first made the pavlova or the pikelet isn't really a war at all. In Australia we love to drag out and rehash this old losing battle every so often, but in New Zealand they couldn't give a hoot. They know it was them, and they're going to keep making them. And they're going to taste pretty damn good, too.

Pages 188–9: The hills around the Bay of Plenty, North Island
Top left: Among the vines in the Gibbston Valley, Otago, South Island
Top right: The Kawarau River, South Island
Bottom left: Putting down a hangi, Rotorua, North Island
Bottom right: Cooking crayfish in Kaikoura, South Island

The secret behind a good whitebait patty (or whitebait fritter, depending on which coast of New Zealand you are on) is concentrating on the whitebait. It doesn't need flour or any other fillers, just a touch of egg to hold the whitebait together and that's it. It's more of an omelette than a patty, really.

These are delicious with white bread or rolls, slathered with plenty of butter; smoked butter is a particularly good match.

WHITEBAIT PATTIES WITH MINTED SALAD

PREPARATION 10 MINUTES
COOKING 15 MINUTES
SERVES 4

500 g whitebait (see Note)

2 eggs

1 cup (250 ml) vegetable oil

60 g ghee (optional)

lemon wedges, to serve

buttered soft white rolls,
     to serve

MINTED SALAD

2 large handfuls of torn
     baby cos lettuce

1 avocado, sliced

1 cup torn mint leaves

½ cup (30 g) alfalfa sprouts

½ cup (125 g) thick yoghurt

½ teaspoon honey

2 tablespoons lemon juice

¼ teaspoon salt

In a bowl, mix the whitebait and eggs together, gently breaking up the eggs with a spoon.

Heat the oil and ghee, if using, in a large frying pan over high heat. Drop 2 tablespoons of the whitebait mixture into the pan for each patty, and shape them into patties in the pan. Cook for 2 minutes on each side, or until golden, cooked through and crisp around the edges. Drain well on paper towel. Season well with salt and freshly ground pepper.

To make the salad, gently toss the lettuce, avocado, mint and alfalfa sprouts in a large bowl. In a separate bowl, combine the yoghurt, honey, lemon juice and salt and season with black pepper. Drizzle the salad with the dressing and toss to coat.

Serve the whitebait patties with the minted salad, lemon wedges, and buttered soft white rolls.

NOTE Whitebait aren't a specific species of fish but the young of quite a few different species. You need very small whitebait for these patties, no more than 5 cm long and 5 mm wide. Check with your fishmonger as to what they have available.

JOHN YOUNG

JOHN YOUNG LIVES IN PARADISE. HE'D CALL HIMSELF A MUSSEL FARMER,
BUT I THINK WHAT JOHN DOES GOES A LITTLE FURTHER THAN THAT.

He's been instrumental to the thriving success that is the
New Zealand mussel industry, both in terms of inventing some
of the machinery and processes that underpin a sustainable and
environmentally sensitive operation, as well as in his tireless
drive to make the industry the best it can be, from improving
yield all the way through to his dream of putting cans of
New Zealand mussel soup into every vending machine in Japan.

What struck me most about John was the part of his personality
that seems fixated on the goal of improvement. On camera
we spoke about mussels, of course, but off camera the same
philosophy seemed to apply to every aspect of his life – from
designing a boat ramp that automatically pulls his boat out of
the water, to trying to find the best speakers for his music room,
or just making the perfect cup of coffee.

For a guy who says he had difficulty learning at school,
it seems like he's turned the whole world into his school.

John describes his life as 'a boys' own adventure', and when
you think about connecting the lines between adventure,
learning and improvement, you might think of travelling to the
far reaches of the globe to unlock its secrets. But much of John's
adventuring has been in his boat, punting around the pristine
waters of the Marlborough Sounds.

As far as I've travelled in *Destination Flavour*, whenever I think
of John I'm reminded of the one great truth of any journey – that
every adventure is a personal one.

Not every recipe is perfect when I cook it on *Destination Flavour*, but I actually don't mind that. When you have a chance to spend time with experts in their field, it's an amazing opportunity to learn. I first made this dish the way I'd always cooked mussels, in a big pot allowing them to steam open, the way most people would – but after John Young (see page 195) showed me how he does it, I haven't cooked mussels in the old way since.

Here's an updated version of this recipe, which I think really improves the dish.

MUSSELS WITH SAFFRON PICI

PREPARATION 30 MINUTES +
20 MINUTES RESTING
COOKING 20 MINUTES
SERVES 4

100 ml extra-virgin olive oil

4 garlic cloves, finely
   chopped

3 eschallots, finely chopped

3 tomatoes, seeds removed,
   diced

½ cup (125 ml) white wine

1 kg mussels, scrubbed
   clean, beards removed

2 tablespoons finely
   shredded flat-leaf parsley

lemon wedges, to serve

SAFFRON PICI

150 g (1 cup) strong flour,
   plus extra for dusting

a pinch of salt

a pinch of saffron threads,
   soaked in 2 tablespoons
   warm water

To make the pici dough, combine the flour and salt in a bowl and make a well in the centre. Add the saffron threads and their soaking water, then continue to gradually add a further 2–3 tablespoons lukewarm water, mixing with a fork, just until it forms a shaggy dough.

Turn the dough out onto a lightly floured board and knead for about 10 minutes, or until smooth and elastic. Wrap the dough in plastic wrap and rest at room temperature for 20 minutes.

Moisten the palms of your hands with a little water and, working quickly, roll the dough into one long noodle, about 5 mm thick. Lightly dust a board or tray with flour and curl the noodle into a spiral.

Heat the oil in a large pot over medium–low heat. Add the garlic and eschalot and cook for about 5 minutes, stirring until softened and fragrant. Add the tomato and cook for a further 5 minutes, then stir in the wine and simmer until reduced by about half. Turn off the heat.

Bring a large pot of salted water to the boil and add the mussels. (John adds them in an old deep-fryer basket, which helps him pull the mussels out just as they open.) You can cook the mussels in batches if you wish.

As soon as the mussels open (this will only take 2–3 minutes), scoop them out and add them to the pot with the tomato and garlic mixture.

Add the pici to the mussel water and cook for about 3 minutes, or until tender.

Mix the mussels and pici into the sauce over medium heat, with a touch of the mussel-cooking water, until a glossy sauce coats the pici.

Scatter with the parsley and season with freshly ground black pepper. Serve with lemon wedges.

NOTE The beauty of John's technique for cooking mussels is that it allows you to control the texture of the mussels perfectly. Mussels contain two types of 'juice' – the briny sea water inside the shell (which can sometimes be a little dirty or gritty), and the intramuscular liquid in the mussel itself (a kind of mussel stock). By pulling the mussels out of the water as soon as they open, the mussels expel the sea water, but through their residual heat will continue to slowly cook in their own intramuscular broth, retaining all their flavour. It's a great way to cook mussels.

Most of us would associate New Zealand with its lamb, and there sure are a lot of sheep roaming around the country – but in many ways New Zealand has remained closer to its British heritage than Australia has. A good roast beef with gravy and Yorkshire pudding is as much a part of New Zealand cuisine as a leg of lamb might be. Serve with roasted kumara (see page 202) and green peas. If you wish, you can use a muffin tin to make around eight individual Yorkshire puddings, instead of one big one.

SUNDAY ROAST BEEF WITH GRAVY & A BIG YORKSHIRE PUDDING

PREPARATION 30 MINUTES
COOKING 1 HOUR 10 MINUTES
SERVES 4–6

1–1.5 kg beef rump cap (picanha)

1 tablespoon olive oil

3 carrots, halved lengthways

1 large onion, roughly chopped

2 tablespoons plain flour

2 cups (500 ml) good-quality beef stock

1 teaspoon sherry vinegar

ROSEMARY & PEPPER RUB

2 tablespoons black peppercorns

1 teaspoon salt

4 garlic cloves, bruised

2 tablespoons dijon mustard

75 g butter, softened

3 rosemary sprigs (or kawakawa, if available)

BIG YORKSHIRE PUDDING

4 × 50 g eggs

200 ml milk

a pinch of salt

1⅓ cups (200 g) plain flour

⅔ cup (170 ml) beef dripping, lard or vegetable oil

Heat your oven to 180°C. For the pepper rub, coarsely grind the pepper, salt and garlic using a mortar and pestle. Transfer to a bowl and mix well with the remaining ingredients.

Using a sharp knife, score the fat cap of the beef. Heat a large roasting tin over high heat and add the oil. Season the beef all over with salt and sear on all sides, turning until browned all over.

Add the carrot and onion to the roasting tin and place the beef on top. Brush the beef well with the pepper rub. Roast for 25–35 minutes, or until the internal temperature reaches 50°C for medium-rare. Transfer the beef to a tray, cover with foil and set aside to rest for 15–20 minutes.

To make the Yorkshire pudding batter, whisk together the eggs, milk and salt until smooth. Sift in the flour and whisk until just combined. Strain the mixture into a large jug and rest in the fridge for 30 minutes.

Increase the oven temperature to 220°C. Pour the dripping into a 20 cm pie dish and heat in the oven for 10 minutes. Without removing the dish from the oven, pour the batter into the hot oil. Bake for 25 minutes, or until the Yorkshire pudding is puffed and golden.

To make the gravy, discard any excess oil from the beef roasting tin. Place the pan with the roasted vegetables back over medium–high heat. Add the flour, stirring well. Gently mash up the roasted vegetables, then cook for 6–8 minutes, or until the flour is golden. Deglaze the pan with about one-third of the beef stock, scraping the bottom of the pan with the spoon. Stir in the remaining stock and any resting juices, and cook for a further 1–2 minutes, or until heated through. Strain through a sieve, season with salt, and stir in the vinegar.

Serve the beef with the Yorkshire pudding and gravy, with peas and roasted kumara on the side.

NOTE When I made this dish in New Zealand, I used a native herb known as kawakawa. It has a peppery, herbaceous aroma, but is not found outside New Zealand. It's delicious, so if you can get your hands on it, give it a go. Otherwise, use rosemary instead.

A quiet
moment near
Whakatane,
North Island

Kumara are a national treasure in New Zealand, having been brought by the first Maori settlers from the Pacific. There are many different varieties, with flesh ranging from snow white to deep red. The bright orange Beauregard variety is the most popular, but if you can get your hands on any others, give them a shot.

WHOLE ROAST KUMARA
WITH PERSILLADE & SOUR CREAM

PREPARATION 10 MINUTES +
15 MINUTES RESTING
COOKING 1 HOUR
SERVES 4

4 orange-fleshed kumara or
　sweet potato, scrubbed
　but not peeled

sour cream, to serve

PERSILLADE

3 tablespoons finely
　shredded parsley

2 garlic cloves, finely
　chopped

2 tablespoons olive oil

1 tablespoon lemon juice

a pinch of salt

Heat your oven to 190°C. Line a baking dish with baking paper.

Prick each kumara all over with a fork, place in the baking dish and roast for 45 minutes to 1 hour, or until tender when gently squeezed; use an oven mitt while squeezing the kumara, so as not to burn your hand.

Remove the kumara from the oven and allow to rest for at least 15 minutes; this resting will convert more starch to sugar, making the potatoes sweeter.

For the persillade, combine the ingredients in a bowl and mix well.

Split each kumara lengthways and dollop with sour cream. Sprinkle with the persillade to serve.

NOTE 'Kumara' is the Maori word for the vegetable known elsewhere as sweet potato. While there are many different varieties, kumara and sweet potato are essentially the same thing.

I'll level with you: sometimes the dishes I choose to cook on *Destination Flavour* are just to see if I can do them. Literally meaning 'eat lobster' in the local language, Kaikoura in New Zealand's South Island is a lobster lover's paradise, and not too far from Kaikoura is the French settlement of Akaroa.

Inspired by these two places, I wanted to make a classic French lobster dish, but all we had to cook on was a campfire. One of our crew joked that I should make a lobster thermidor, and I thought 'Bloody hell, I'll give it a go!'

CAMPFIRE LOBSTER THERMIDOR

PREPARATION 20 MINUTES +
COAL/BARBECUE HEATING
COOKING 45 MINUTES
SERVES 6

3 × 800 g raw lobsters, halved lengthways, cleaned

1 cup (250 ml) white wine

¼ cup (60 ml) Cognac

¼ cup (30 g) finely chopped eschalot

1 bunch tarragon, around 10 small sprigs

1 tablespoon dijon mustard

¼ cup (25 g) finely grated parmesan

toasted and buttered baguette slices, to serve

ENRICHED BÉCHAMEL SAUCE

½ brown onion, peeled

6 cloves

2 cups (500 ml) milk

2 bay leaves

75 g butter

2 tablespoons plain flour

1 egg yolk

a pinch of ground nutmeg

Build a campfire and allow it to burn down to hot coals. Alternatively, heat a barbecue to medium heat.

Put the lobster halves, cut side up, on the coals or barbecue, then cook for 5–7 minutes on each side, or until the meat is lightly cooked and easily comes away from the shell. Remove the meat from the shells and cut it into large pieces; reserve the shells for serving.

To make the béchamel sauce, stud the onion half with the cloves and add to a saucepan with the milk and bay leaves. Bring the milk to just below boiling point, then remove from the heat and set aside for a few minutes. In another saucepan, melt the butter over medium heat until foaming, then add the flour and stir for 2 minutes, or until the mixture resembles wet sand but has not taken on any colour. Gradually add the warm milk, stirring until smooth and thickened. Cook, stirring, for a further 2 minutes, then remove from the heat. Stir in the egg yolk and nutmeg and season with salt and pepper. Set aside until needed.

To finish the dish, combine the wine, Cognac, eschalot and tarragon in a saucepan over medium–high heat. Cook for about 5 minutes, or until reduced to about 2 tablespoons liquid. Discard the tarragon, then add the mixture to the béchamel sauce, along with the mustard, and stir to combine. Fold the lobster meat through.

Fill the lobster shells with the lobster mixture and scatter with the parmesan. Place on a large metal tray under an overhead grill for 5 minutes, or until golden and heated through. If doing this on a campfire, brûlée the lobster with a blowtorch.

Serve the lobsters with the buttered toasts and a fresh garden salad.

NOTE To humanely dispatch a live lobster, chill it to nearly freezing, either in a freezer or in iced water, then split it in half lengthways. The lobster's 'brain' is actually a series of nodes distributed throughout the body, so splitting it in half completely is one of the most humane ways to kill it.

It may not have looked like it on camera, but this was one of those days when whatever could go wrong did. It was summer in New Zealand, so I thought I would go fly fishing in shorts. As it turned out, there was an unseasonal cold snap and it actually started snowing for a few minutes.

Then we only had one pair of waders. I said I'd just go into the water in my pants, which were green and would look like waders for you folks watching on TV, so we wouldn't have to waste two hours getting back to town for a second set of waders. I figured we'd catch a fish in a few minutes and no-one would be the wiser – but it took us hours to catch a fish, and I don't think I've ever felt so cold in my life. Our cameraman was actually bedridden for a few days afterwards and I wasn't far behind!

Then, when we set ourselves on the bank to start cooking, wouldn't you know it, it began bucketing down with rain, so we had to pack everything up and head back to our wet weather location to actually cook the fish! The only saving graces that day were that we caught a fish, and that it tasted pretty bloody great. I look back on it now as a great memory, but boy did we earn it!

BROWN TROUT
WITH BUTTER, CIDER & LENTILS

PREPARATION 15 MINUTES
COOKING 35 MINUTES
SERVES 4

1 small lemon, thinly sliced

1 whole brown or rainbow trout, cleaned

½ small onion, thinly sliced

sea salt, for seasoning

⅓ cup (90 g butter), softened

½ cup (125 ml) cider

flat-leaf parsley leaves, to garnish

BRAISED LENTILS

1 tablespoon butter

50 g speck or pancetta, cut into batons

1 small onion, cut into 5 mm pieces

1 small carrot, cut into 5 mm pieces

1 celery stalk, cut into 5 mm pieces

2 cups (370 g) dried French green lentils

1 bay leaf

4 cups (1 litre) chicken or vegetable stock

For the braised lentils, melt the butter in a large saucepan over medium heat. Add the speck and cook for about 3 minutes, stirring regularly until lightly browned. Add the onion, carrot and celery and cook for a further 5 minutes, until the vegetables are slightly softened. Add the lentils to the pan, stirring to coat them in the mixture, then add the bay leaf and stock. Bring to the boil, then reduce the heat and simmer for 15–20 minutes, or until the lentils are just tender, adding a little water to the pan if it starts to look dry during cooking. Season to taste with salt and black pepper.

Heat your oven to 200°C. Lay two large pieces of foil on a flat surface and place a few lemon slices in the centre. Place the fish on top of the lemon and stuff the fish with the onion and some more lemon slices. Place the remaining lemon slices on top, then season the fish with sea salt. Place knobs of butter on top of the fish, and inside the cavity. Start to fold the foil into a parcel, pour in the cider, then tightly enclose the fish with the foil. Place on a large baking tray and roast for 15 minutes, or until the fish is just cooked through.

Transfer the lentils to a serving platter. Carefully unwrap the fish and place on top of the lentils. Drizzle with the buttery cider sauce and garnish with parsley leaves to serve.

NOTE You might have seen green lentils called 'Puy lentils', but actually they should only be called that if they are actually from the Le Puy region in France. It's an AOC (appellation d'origine contrôlée – protected designation of origin) term throughout Europe, just like the sparkling wines from Champagne.

HANS BIEMOND

I UMMED AND AHHED OVER WHETHER TO INCLUDE THIS PICTURE IN THIS BOOK, AND I'M GUESSING BY LOOKING AT IT YOU CAN SEE WHY.

For those of us who eat animals, their death is a necessary part of how we live. We can hide it from our daily lives by pretending that the neatly wrapped packages of meat in our supermarkets aren't produced by an ultimate brutality done in our name. But it just isn't true.

Over the years in *Destination Flavour*, we've tried to show the truth of food. I can't tell you how many angry letters I've received from people upset that I, smiling, pulled a crab or lobster from the water for a meal, or met a pig before I ultimately cooked it. It sits uncomfortably with people when that reality we try to hide is juxtaposed so closely with behaviour that could easily be their own. I don't blame anyone for how they feel about an issue that is so obviously emotional. Euphemisms like 'beef' and 'pork' persist in our language mainly because they divorce the living cow or pig from its sad end upon the dining table.

Hans Biemond arrived in New Zealand from Holland in 1984, and for more than thirty years he's fed his family of ten with deer, hares, pigs, rabbits, turkeys and ducks hunted out of the hills surrounding his property.

For Hans there is no hiding from the truth. When I met him his hands were quite literally covered with the blood of an animal that would feed his children for the next week.

I included this photo here for the same reason I have tried to champion the ethical treatment of animals and sustainable management of our food resources for my entire career. We have to care about it. We have to be emotional about it.

If we willingly suspend our knowledge that our life comes from an animal's death, then we take less ownership of ensuring that its life and death occur on humane terms. For all meat eaters, we need images like this and experiences like this to remind ourselves of our responsibility for our food.

If this image angers you, I apologise. That truly is not my intention. But perhaps you should also ask yourself why this angers you more than the picture of the pie on the next page, for one surely follows from the other.

Developing this dish, I wanted to create something that summed up much of the South Island of New Zealand for me. It's a wild, abundant place, but it moves at its own leisurely pace. The whole area is fragrant with wild thyme, and the mountains are rich with game. This dish takes only meats hunted in the area and combines them in a rich game stew. Topped with kumara and an Irish potato champ, the shepherds can keep their lamb – this is a Hunter's Pie. Use farmed venison if wild deer is unavailable.

NEW ZEALAND HUNTER'S PIE

PREPARATION 30 MINUTES + AT LEAST 4 HOURS MARINATING
COOKING ABOUT 6 HOURS
SERVES 8

500 g wild deer leg meat, cut into 5 cm cubes

1 wild deer shank

1 wild hare, skinned and jointed, or substitute rabbit

1 brown onion, peeled

1 small carrot, peeled

1 celery stalk

1 apple

1 bouquet garni of 10 wild thyme sprigs, 3 rosemary sprigs, 1 small bunch flat-leaf parsley and 2 bay leaves

6 garlic cloves, peeled

1 teaspoon ground white pepper

½ teaspoon ground nutmeg

¼ teaspoon ground cloves

750 ml pinot noir

1 wild pork hock

¼ cup (60 g) butter, diced

¼ cup (60 ml) olive oil

plain flour, for dusting

1 pig's trotter

3 tomatoes, chopped

12–15 pearl onions

kumara mash, potato champ, brown butter and parsley, to serve

Place the venison pieces and hare in a deep dish or bowl and grate over the onion, carrot, celery and apple. Add the bouquet garni, along with the garlic and ground spices. Pour in the wine and mix to combine. Cover and marinate in the fridge for at least 4 hours, or preferably overnight.

Place the pork hock in a saucepan and cover with cold water. Bring to the boil, then reduce the heat to a simmer and cook for 2 hours. Remove the pork from the stock and set aside to cool, reserving 6 cups (1.5 litres) of the stock.

Working in batches, heat the butter and oil in a large heavy-based saucepan over medium–high heat. Place the flour in a shallow tray. Drain and reserve the marinade from the venison and hare, then dust the meat lightly in the flour, shaking off any excess. Cook the meat for 5 minutes, turning, until browned. Remove and set aside.

Pour the marinade into the pan and bring to the boil over medium–high heat. Using a large spoon, skim off any impurities that rise to the surface. Add the venison, hare, pork hock, pig's trotter and tomatoes. Pour in the reserved pork stock and bring to the boil. Reduce the heat to medium–low and simmer for 2–3 hours, or until all the meats are tender. Remove the meat from the stock and shred, discarding the bones.

Place the pan back over medium heat. Add the pearl onions and bring to the boil. Cook at a simmer for 20 minutes, or until the sauce is reduced and glossy, and the onions are tender. Return the shredded meat to the pan and stir to combine, then cook for a final 10 minutes, or until heated through. Season to taste with salt and pepper.

Top the stew with kumara mash and potato champ. Drizzle with brown butter and grill the top of the dish under a very hot overhead grill until lightly browned. Scatter with parsley and serve.

NOTE You could easily adapt this recipe to just use beef, or lamb, or venison, or a combination of them. Perhaps even try Australian game. Kangaroo and emu would work well together with some pancetta and chuck steak. You could even use game sausages for a simple shortcut.

We always focus on the pavlova as the great battleground between Australian and New Zealand cuisine, but it could just as easily be the pikelet. Originally adapted from Scottish drop scones, just like the pavlova it's likely the pikelet came first from New Zealand, as a delicious contrast to thin British-style pancakes. Matched with a bit of kiwi fruit jam and cream, it's a beautiful New Zealand breakfast or afternoon tea.

YOGHURT PIKELETS WITH KIWI FRUIT JAM

PREPARATION 20 MINUTES + AT LEAST 30 MINUTES RESTING
COOKING 35 MINUTES FOR THE JAM, 4–5 MINUTES FOR EACH BATCH OF PIKELETS
MAKES ABOUT 12 PIKELETS AND 3 CUPS JAM

1 egg

1½ tablespoons caster sugar

1½ cups (375 g) plain yoghurt

1 cup (150 g) plain flour

1 teaspoon bicarbonate of soda

a few tablespoons of milk (optional)

1 tablespoon melted butter, plus extra for brushing

thick cream, to serve

2 tablespoons icing sugar, for dusting (optional)

KIWI FRUIT JAM

1 kg kiwi fruit

juice of 3 lemons

1½ cups (335 g) caster sugar

For the jam, scoop the flesh from the kiwi fruit and place in a saucepan. Add the lemon juice and cook over medium–high heat for 10 minutes. Add the sugar and ½ cup (125 ml) water, stirring to dissolve the sugar. Simmer for a further 25 minutes, or until the mixture has a jam-like consistency, stirring occasionally. Ladle into sterilised jars and allow to cool completely; the jam will keep in the fridge for up to 2 months.

To make the pikelets, whisk the egg, sugar and yoghurt in a bowl until smooth. Sift the flour and bicarbonate of soda into the bowl, and fold gently until just combined. Depending on the thickness of the yoghurt, you can add a few tablespoons of milk for a thinner batter, if you prefer. Cover with a tea towel and rest in the fridge for at least 30 minutes, although I often leave the batter to rest overnight.

When you're ready to cook, gently fold the melted butter through the pikelet batter, and set a large frying pan over medium–low heat. In batches, lightly brush the pan with melted butter. Spoon 2 tablespoons of the batter per pikelet into the pan. Cook for about 2 minutes on each side, or until golden and cooked through.

Serve the pikelets immediately, with the kiwi fruit jam and a little cream, all dusted with a light fall of icing sugar, if desired.

NOTE I am not awfully fussy when it comes to the setting of jam, but if you want to see whether the jam is set just use the plate test. Chill a plate in the freezer for at least 5 minutes, then drop a teaspoon of jam onto it and return it to the freezer for a further 2 minutes. If the jam on the plate forms a skin that wrinkles when you push it with your finger, it will set. Personally I don't mind a jam that is less set, as the runny consistency is perfect for serving with dishes like pikelets.

The key to this dish is simplicity, as it aims to extract the purest strawberry flavour from the berries, both in the form of juice and the roasted strawberry flesh. A touch of aniseed in the cream enhances the strawberry flavour even more. If this is your first attempt at a moulded jelly, opt for a thin metal or plastic mould, or even a flexible silicone mould. Older, ornate and heavier ceramic or glass moulds can be difficult to turn out.

STRAWBERRY JELLY
WITH ROASTED STRAWBERRY & ANISE FOOL

PREPARATION 10 MINUTES + AT LEAST 4 HOURS DRAINING + 4 HOURS SETTING
COOKING 50 MINUTES
SERVES 4–6

5½ cups (1 kg) strawberries, hulled and chopped, plus extra to serve

100 g caster sugar

1 tablespoon white vinegar

10 gelatine leaves or 25 g powdered gelatine

200 ml thickened cream

2 tablespoons Pernod, or other anise-flavoured liqueur

Place the strawberries, sugar and vinegar in a saucepan set over very low heat. Lightly mash the strawberries to release their juice. Gently heat for 30 minutes, stirring occasionally, taking care not to allow the mixture to boil or steam; you may need to keep turning the heat on and off.

Line a fine sieve with layers of muslin, and set it over a large bowl. Pour the strawberry mixture into the sieve, then place in the fridge for at least 4 hours, or preferably overnight, to allow the juice to drip through slowly into the bowl.

Reserving the pulp in the sieve, pour the strawberry liquor into a large jug and top up with enough water to make 4 cups (1 litre).

Place the gelatine leaves in a bowl and cover with cold water. Set aside for a few minutes until softened.

Pour the strawberry liquor into a saucepan and gently heat it through over medium–low heat. Squeeze the excess water out of the gelatine leaves and add them to the strawberry liquor, whisking until fully dissolved.

Strain the mixture through a fine sieve, into a 4 cup (1 litre) jelly mould. Chill in the fridge for about 4 hours, or until set.

Heat your oven to 200°C. Spread the reserved strawberry pulp over a lined baking tray and bake for 15 minutes, or until nicely caramelised. Remove from the oven and allow to cool completely.

For the strawberry and anise fool, whip the cream and Pernod to stiff peaks, then fold the cooled strawberry pulp through.

To serve, place the jelly mould in a large pan of hot water for about 1 minute, to release the jelly from the mould.

Invert the jelly onto a platter. Serve with the strawberry fool and extra strawberries.

NOTE Different brands of gelatine leaves vary in strength. Check the strength of your gelatine leaves to ensure you are using the right quantity to produce a firm jelly in 4 cups (1 litre) of liquid.

SINGAPORE

You could say that Singapore breaks all the rules of modern food.

With so much focus in the rest of the world on seasonality and agriculturally driven produce, how does a country without clearly defined seasons and little agriculture to speak of make a global case for its food culture? Surprisingly, a look at Singaporean cuisine could be a considered case study in what truly makes a food culture great. →

What Singapore does have is people, dedicated and proud, who celebrate their identity through food. The near-fanatical verve with which Singaporeans embrace their own cuisine might be seen as stronger than even the most breathless advocates of French gastronomy, or the most militant Italian traditionalists.

With Singapore being a young country gaining its independence only in the 1960s, its cuisine has been a touchstone for a national identity, and eating is without doubt the single, unifying national pastime. Singaporeans are fanatical about their food, and barely a conversation in the country can pass without turning to the subject at some point. Have you eaten? What shall we eat next? Can we eat now?

Luckily, in the food lover's paradise of Singapore, all of those questions are easily answered.

Pages 216–7: A pool with a view at Marina Bay Sands
Top left: Breaking the Ramadan fast for Hari Raya Aidilfitri
Top right: Colourful flower garlands in Little India
Bottom left: Rolina's Hainanese curry puffs, Tanjong Pagar Food Centre
Bottom middle: Durian, rambutan, mangosteen and jackfruit for sale in Geylang
Bottom right: A hawker centre feast

Satays are one of my favourite foods, but they aren't something you should make alone. Gather friends and family around and let their many hands make light work of the task. In my family, so many stories have been shared across a table while we all sit around threading hundreds of satays onto skewers.

CHICKEN SATAY

PREPARATION 1 HOUR + OVERNIGHT MARINATING + 20 MINUTES SOAKING + BARBECUE HEATING
COOKING 30 MINUTES
MAKES ABOUT 75 SKEWERS

1.5 kg skinless, boneless chicken thighs
peanut oil, for brushing
cucumber and onion, to serve

MARINADE

1 small brown onion, roughly chopped
3 garlic cloves, peeled
2 cm piece of fresh ginger, peeled and chopped
3 lemongrass stems, inner core only, finely sliced
2 tablespoons ground coriander
1 tablespoon ground cumin
1 teaspoon ground fennel
1 teaspoon ground turmeric
¼ cup (55 g) sugar
1 teaspoon salt
1 tablespoon soy sauce
¼ cup (60 ml) peanut oil

PEANUT SAUCE

10 large dried chillies
2 brown onions, sliced
4 garlic cloves, peeled
2 lemongrass stems, inner core only, finely sliced
1 tablespoon belacan (shrimp paste)
1 teaspoon ground coriander
1 teaspoon ground cumin
¼ cup (60 ml) peanut oil
400 ml tin coconut milk
1 tablespoon tamarind paste
2 tablespoons sugar
1 teaspoon salt
1¾ cups (250 g) ground roasted peanuts

Cut the chicken into 2.5 cm cubes. For the marinade, combine all the ingredients in a blender or food processor and purée. Cover the chicken with the mixture. Cover and marinate in the fridge overnight.

Thread the marinated chicken onto soaked bamboo skewers; the skewers should hold each piece tightly. You can thread each piece more than once to hold it in place if necessary. Finish each skewer with a grabbing motion, to press the chicken close to the skewer.

For the peanut sauce, soak the chillies in hot water for 20 minutes. Combine the chillies, onion, garlic, lemongrass, belacan, coriander and cumin in a blender and blend to a purée.

Heat the peanut oil in a saucepan over medium–low heat and fry the blended paste for about 10–15 minutes, stirring frequently, until very fragrant. Stir in 1 cup (250 ml) water and the coconut milk and bring to a simmer. Mix the tamarind paste with ½ cup (125 ml) hot water, then add the tamarind water, sugar and salt to the pan and simmer for a further 5 minutes, until the sauce starts to form an oily gloss on the surface. Stir the peanuts through and simmer for a further 5 minutes, until thickened. You can add a little more water if necessary to maintain the consistency. Taste and adjust the seasoning if necessary.

Grill the satays on a hot barbecue, basting regularly with peanut oil and turning regularly, for about 5 minutes, or until cooked through.

Serve the satays with the peanut sauce, and some chopped cucumber and onion.

NOTE Don't throw out the woody stalks of the lemongrass. Their texture makes them unsuitable for eating, but they still have great flavour. Bash them to loosen the fibres and tie them together to make a brush for brushing the satays, or boil them with fresh ginger and galangal in a sugar syrup to make a delicious cordial.

I have been making Hainanese chicken rice for more than twenty years, and my method has changed a bit during all that time. I learned first from my grandmother, Chew Kwei-Eng, who made this dish for me thousands of times, and from my mother, Dr Joyce Hill, whose old cookbook from the 1970s sets out her handwritten recipe for the chilli sauce. I've also picked up a few things from people on my travels – like my cousin, Liow Tong Thong, who was born in Hainan, but ran a chicken rice stall in Singapore for forty years. (He's more than thirty years older than I am but we're considered cousins as we're from the same generation of the Liaw clan.)

Recipes are works in progress and, although this recipe is how I make my chicken rice now, it might well change in the future. All good recipes should.

HAINANESE CHICKEN RICE

PREPARATION 15 MINUTES
COOKING 2 HOURS
SERVES 4–6

1.7 kg whole chicken, at room temperature

5 cm piece of fresh ginger, unpeeled

2 teaspoons salt

½ teaspoon monosodium glutamate (MSG) or 1 teaspoon chicken stock powder (optional)

1 tablespoon sesame oil

coriander, to serve

sliced cucumber, to serve

Chilli sauce for chicken (page 232), to serve

GINGER & SPRING ONION OIL

2 tablespoons grated fresh ginger

½ teaspoon sea salt flakes

4 spring onions, thinly sliced, green tops reserved

¼ cup (60 ml) peanut oil

For the ginger and spring onion oil, pound the ginger and salt to a rough paste using a heatproof mortar and pestle. Add the thinly sliced spring onion and pound lightly to combine. Heat the peanut oil in a small frying pan until it is smoking then pour the hot oil over the ginger mixture. Stir, then set aside until ready to serve.

Remove the fat deposits from inside the cavity of the chicken, near the tail. Roughly chop the fat and place in a small frying pan over very low heat. Render the chicken fat, stirring occasionally, for about 1 hour, until all the fat is rendered to liquid and the solids are crisp. Remove the solids and use them for another purpose; they're great mixed into fried noodles. Reserve the chicken oil.

Pound the ginger using a mortar and pestle, then add to a large pot containing about 16 cups (4 litres) water, along with the reserved spring onion greens from the ginger and spring onion oil. Add the salt and MSG, if using, and bring to the boil over high heat. Taste the water and adjust the amount of salt, so that it tastes savoury and a little salty. Reduce the heat to very low and carefully add the chicken to the pan, breast side down. There should be enough water that the chicken doesn't touch the bottom, as that will cause the skin to tear. The water should be steaming but not bubbling. Keep the heat at this level and cook the chicken for 45 minutes.

Reserving the stock in the pot, use a poultry hook to carefully lift the chicken out, ensuring you don't break the skin, and plunge it straight into a large bowl or sink of salted iced water. Leave the chicken in the iced water for at least 10 minutes, turning once. This will stop the cooking process and give the skin its delicious gelatinous texture.

Remove the chicken from the iced water and hang over a bowl or the sink to drain well. Rub the skin all over with the sesame oil. The chicken should be cooked very lightly, and pink inside the bones, with a gelatinous skin.

CHICKEN RICE

3⅓ cups (665 g) jasmine rice

3 tablespoons vegetable oil, approximately

4 garlic cloves, bruised

3 cm piece of fresh ginger, unpeeled and bruised

2 eschalots, roughly sliced

DRESSING

1 tablespoon sesame oil

2 tablespoons light soy sauce

To make the chicken rice, place the rice in a rice cooker or heavy-based saucepan. Combine the rendered chicken oil with enough vegetable oil to make ½ cup (125 ml), then warm it in a wok over medium heat. Add the garlic, ginger and eschalot and stir until starting to brown. Strain the oil, discarding the solids, and add it to the rice with 1.2 litres of the reserved (and strained) stock from the chicken. Bring to the boil over high heat and continue to boil for about 5 minutes, or until the level of the liquid reaches the top of the rice. Reduce the heat to very low, cover with a tight-fitting lid and cook for 12 minutes. Remove from the heat and stand for another 10 minutes.

Combine the dressing ingredients with about another ½ cup (125 ml) of the reserved chicken stock.

When the rice is ready, use a cleaver to slice and debone the chicken Chinese-style and pour the dressing over it. Scatter with coriander sprigs, and serve with the rice, sliced cucumber, the ginger and spring onion oil, and chilli sauce.

NOTE The key to a good chicken rice is making a strong, savoury stock, as that will ensure the chicken, rice and chilli sauce all have enough taste. MSG is a popular additive but is by no means necessary, as you can make a good chicken rice just by using salted water or stock. I will sometimes even use a light Japanese dashi, or even just add a lug of strongly savoury fish sauce to the water, in place of MSG.

This page, top left: Me and my mum, Dr Joyce Hill AO **Top right:** My grandmother, Chew Kwei-Eng, and my daughter, Anna
Bottom: My cousin Liow Tong Thong
Opposite: Hainanese chicken rice (page 222)

This might well be considered Singapore's national dish, and it's much easier to prepare than you might imagine. Pick your way through the crab and use the crispy and fluffy deep-fried mantou to mop up the delicious sauce. This is a dish as much about the texture as it is about the taste.

SINGAPORE CHILLI CRAB

PREPARATION 20 MINUTES +
30 MINUTES FREEZING
COOKING 30 MINUTES
SERVES 2–4

1 large mud crab

¼ cup (60 ml) vegetable oil

¼ teaspoon salt

1 cup (250 ml) tomato passata

2 cups (500 ml) chicken stock or water

2 tablespoons palm sugar

1 tablespoon white vinegar

1 tablespoon soy sauce

2 tablespoons tomato ketchup

5 thin spring onions, cut into 5 cm lengths

2 teaspoons cornflour, mixed with 2 tablespoons cold water

1 egg, beaten

½ cup coriander leaves

1 bird's eye chilli, sliced

deep-fried mantou (Chinese steamed buns), to serve (optional)

REMPAH

4 eschalots or 1 onion, peeled and sliced

4 garlic cloves, peeled

6 large red chillies, stems removed and seeded

1 teaspoon belacan (shrimp paste)

To prepare your crab humanely, place it in the freezer or submerge in an ice bath for 30 minutes.

Pull the top shell (carapace) away from the body. Discard the feathery gills, but reserve any of the yellowish tomalley from the head. Twist off the claws, then divide the body into four pieces, with two legs on each piece.

Blend the ingredients for the rempah to a smooth paste.

Heat a wok over medium heat and add the oil. Fry the rempah for about 10 minutes, stirring regularly, until the mixture is fragrant and the oil separates from the solids.

Add the crab pieces (including the shell) and salt, and toss for about 2 minutes, until the crab starts to change colour.

Add the passata, stock, palm sugar, vinegar, soy sauce and ketchup and toss to coat. Stir in the spring onion and any crab tomalley, then cover the wok and simmer for 10 minutes.

Taste the sauce and adjust its seasoning and consistency. Transfer the crab to a serving plate.

Drizzle enough of the cornflour mixture slowly into the wok while stirring to slightly thicken the sauce, then drizzle the beaten egg slowly into the wok while stirring, to create threads of egg through the sauce.

Spoon the sauce over the crab, scatter with coriander and sliced chilli, and serve immediately, with the fried mantou, if using.

NOTE The process of balancing the taste and consistency of the sauce is all important, as the evaporation from a wok will vary from kitchen to kitchen and wok to wok. A thin, watery sauce will be unpleasant, and a sauce that is too thick will overpower the crab. The taste, too, should be a good balance of savouriness from the crab, tomato and belacan, sourness from the vinegar, and sweetness from the sugar and ketchup.

Just about every family in Singapore (and Malaysia and Indonesia) will have their own rendang recipe. Some rendangs will be dry and thick, others wet with gravy. Some will include powdered hard spices like cumin and coriander seeds, and barks such as cinnamon, and others won't. Some will include kerisik (the caramelised coconut) to thicken the sauce, and others will leave it out.

This is how we make rendang in my family – dry-ish with just a small amount of thick gravy, very fragrant from turmeric, galangal and ginger instead of from hard spices, and toasty with kerisik.

BEEF RENDANG

PREPARATION 30 MINUTES
COOKING 4 HOURS
SERVES 8

¼ cup (60 ml) vegetable oil or coconut oil

2 kg beef chuck steak, cut into 5–7 cm pieces, or 3 kg beef short ribs

400 ml tin coconut cream

3 lemongrass stems, fat white stalks only, bruised

3 kaffir lime leaves, plus extra shredded lime leaves to garnish

1 piece of cassia bark

2 star anise

1 tablespoon caster sugar

2 teaspoons salt

1 cup (90 g) desiccated coconut

REMPAH

2 medium-sized onions, or 8 eschalots

5 cm piece of fresh turmeric

5 cm piece of fresh galangal

5 cm piece of fresh ginger

4 garlic cloves, peeled

2–6 bird's eye chillies (to taste), stalks removed

To make the rempah, peel and roughly chop the onions, turmeric, galangal and ginger and place in a blender. Add the peeled garlic cloves and chillies and blend to a purée, adding a little water to help it blend, if necessary.

Heat the oil in a large, heavy-based flameproof casserole dish over medium heat and fry the rempah paste for 15–30 minutes, stirring occasionally at the beginning, and constantly as it thickens, so that it doesn't splatter or catch on the base of the pan. The rempah is ready when it is browned, fragrant and thick.

Add the beef and toss to coat in the rempah. Then add the coconut cream, and enough water to cover the meat. Add the lemongrass, whole lime leaves, cassia, star anise, sugar and salt. Bring to a simmer, then cover and simmer for about 2 hours, until the beef starts to become tender.

Remove the lid and simmer for about 1 hour more, until the stewing liquid has reduced to a thick, oily sauce.

Heat a dry frying pan over medium–low heat. Fry the coconut, stirring constantly, for about 5 minutes, or until it is a deep golden brown. This caramelised coconut is known as kerisik.

Add the kerisik to the rendang, stirring to combine. Simmer for a further 30 minutes or so, until the mixture is deep brown, oily and thick.

The rendang can be eaten straight away but will benefit from being covered and left overnight to allow the flavours to develop.

Serve scattered with finely shredded lime leaves.

TIP A rendang isn't really a curry, although it does follow many of the same principles. In a curry the balance of spices is paramount, but a rendang is defined more by the fragrant rempah and thick coconut gravy than by any hard spices used.

Hainanese cooks like my grandfather were – and still are – legendary around Singapore and Malaysia for their ability to creatively mix the diverse cuisines of the region. Hainanese chicken rice took a traditional dish from Hainan island and adapted it for local ingredients to create a dish that was accessible to all Singaporeans of Chinese, Malay, Indian and European heritage alike – while Hainanese curry rice combined Malay and Indian curried dishes in a Chinese form.

I think kaya toast, however, might be the Hainanese community's greatest contribution to Singapore's food scene. They took kaya, a kind of coconut curd or jam found around Asia, and boosted the flavour with dark caramel, combining it with toast and hand-roasted coffee for a local interpretation of English jam and bread, and in doing so created the original Singaporean coffee shop experience.

KAYA TOAST

PREPARATION 30 MINUTES
COOKING ABOUT 1 HOUR
MAKES ABOUT 4 CUPS (1 LITRE)
OF KAYA

sliced white or wholemeal
  bread, to serve

thick slices of butter,
  to serve

KAYA
10 eggs

3¼ cups (750 g) caster
  sugar

5 pandan leaves, tied in
  a knot

400 ml tin coconut cream
  (see Note)

¼ teaspoon salt

CARAMEL
¼ cup (50 g) caster sugar

1 tablespoon butter

For the kaya, combine the eggs and sugar in a tall, slender saucepan. With a hand whisk, slowly stir in one direction for about 20 minutes, or until the sugar is dissolved – don't lift the whisk out, as that will create air bubbles.

Bring a large saucepan of water to a simmer, and place a tea towel in the bottom of the pan. Place the taller pot into the water and slowly stir for another 5 minutes, to ensure the mixture is fully dissolved.

Add the pandan leaves and coconut cream and stir often for about 30 minutes to 1 hour (or more) until thickened. The time it takes your kaya to thicken will depend on the heat, and also the amount of liquid from the coconut cream (see Note).

To make the caramel, heat the caster sugar in a small saucepan over medium heat until a dark caramel forms. Remove from the heat and stir the butter through.

Add the caramel and salt to the kaya and stir until well combined. Allow to cool, then transfer the kaya to clean jars. The kaya will keep in the fridge for about 3 months.

For the kaya toast, grill two slices of bread for each serve, until well toasted. Cut off the crusts and cover with thick slices of butter. Spread over lots of kaya, sandwich the slices together, cut in half, and serve, preferably with strong Hainanese coffee.

NOTE If using tinned coconut cream, don't shake the can before use. Open the top carefully and scoop out just the thick coconut cream from the top, leaving the watery liquid behind. The volume will be less than 400 ml, but you don't need to top it up as the liquid will just need to be cooked off in the cooking process anyway. Using just the thick portion of the coconut cream will reduce the cooking time.

About ten years ago my mother gave me her old cooking journal, full of handwritten recipes she'd collected over the years. This sauce jumped out at me, as it's one I'd been making for years but never quite managed to get right. In my mother's book she had written the recipe without any measurements at all, and ironically that's what helped me to solve the problem. Instead of trying to follow a recipe for its measurements, I followed it for its taste and, finally, I managed to make this sauce just the way I like it. I've given you measurements here to guide you, but don't feel you need to follow them. As always, mother knows best.

CHILLI SAUCE FOR CHICKEN

PREPARATION 15 MINUTES
COOKING 5 MINUTES
MAKES ABOUT 2 CUPS (500 ML)

4–6 red bird's eye chillies (or to taste), stalks and seeds removed

6 thick slices of peeled fresh ginger

6 garlic cloves, peeled

2 teaspoons caster sugar

½ teaspoon salt

½–1 cup (125–250 ml) chicken stock (such as from making Hainanese chicken rice, page 222)

2 tablespoons calamansi lime juice (from about 6 calamansi limes), or 2 tablespoons lemon juice

2 tablespoons chicken oil (rendered chicken fat; see page 222), or 2 tablespoons peanut oil

Using a mortar and pestle, pound the chillies, ginger, garlic, sugar and salt together until very smooth. Pounding chillies can take some time, so to speed up the process you can start by using a blender or food processor, and pound to finish. (Pounding will improve the flavour and texture of the sauce, as the pounding process seems to aerate and emulsify the sauce, so that the ginger and chilli don't remain separate.)

Bring the stock to the boil in a small saucepan, then pour over the chilli mixture in the mortar. You can vary the amount of stock depending on the consistency of the chilli sauce you're after.

Stir in the lime juice, then adjust the seasoning if necessary, for a pleasant balance of sweet, sour and salty.

Heat the chicken oil in a small saucepan until hot, then pour over the chilli mixture and stir to combine. Transfer the chilli sauce to jars. It will keep in the fridge for about 1 month, but is ready to use immediately.

NOTE Look for the colour of the sauce, rather than following the recipe exactly. It should be a bright orange, and that colour will give you a good indication of the proportion of chilli to ginger. The heat of the sauce should depend on the kind of chillies used, not the amount. The flavour of chilli in this sauce is more important than the heat.

We often think of laksa as just one dish, but travel through Singapore, Malaysia and Indonesia, and you'll find dozens of different varieties – like the sour, mackerel-based Penang laksa, the curry-thick Johor laksa made with dried spaghetti noodles, or even Singapore's home-grown Katong laksa, made with short-cut noodles and eaten as a soup with just a spoon, a little like a minestrone.

The classic coconut milk laksa that we know and love goes by a few different names – Nyonya laksa, laksa lemak, curry laksa or even curry mee – but the key to making it is always the same: rich fragrance from a long-cooked rempah, the slightly gritty texture of ground dried shrimp, a light creaminess from the coconut and a flavour punch from a spoon of sambal.

CHICKEN & PRAWN LAKSA

PREPARATION 1 HOUR + 10 MINUTES STANDING
COOKING 3 HOURS
SERVES 8

1 kg chicken carcasses

1 kg raw, unpeeled large prawns

½ cup (40 g) dried shrimp, soaked in 2 cups (500 ml) hot water for about 20 minutes

¼ cup (60 ml) vegetable oil

2 teaspoons salt

2 teaspoons sugar

1 teaspoon fish sauce

2 × 425 ml tins coconut milk

250 g fried tofu puffs, halved

4 boneless, skinless chicken thighs

1 kg fresh Hokkien noodles

200 g dried rice vermicelli noodles

200 g fried fish cakes, sliced

3⅓ cups (300 g) bean sprouts

8 eggs

1 cup loosely packed Vietnamese mint leaves, finely shredded, to serve

1 Lebanese cucumber, shredded, to serve

Start with the stock. Put the chicken bones in a large saucepan, cover with 10 cups (2.5 litres) water and bring to a low simmer. Gently simmer for about 2 hours, skimming off any scum that rises to the surface.

Peel the prawns, leaving the tails on. Add two-thirds of the shells to the stock and simmer for a further 20 minutes. Stand for at least 10 minutes, then strain, discarding the shells and bones (or reserve for making more stock); reserve the stock. Devein and butterfly the prawns and refrigerate. Grind the dried shrimp to a wet, coarse powder in a small blender, or pound using a mortar and pestle. Set aside.

Blend all the laksa rempah ingredients into a smooth paste.

Heat a large saucepan over medium heat and add the oil. Fry the reserved prawn heads and shells until very fragrant, then remove the shells and heads, leaving the oil in the pan. Add half the laksa rempah (refrigerate the rest for another laksa) and fry for about 10 minutes, stirring frequently, until the oil separates from the paste. Add the reserved chicken stock and bring to a simmer.

Stir in the dried shrimp and its soaking liquid, salt, sugar, fish sauce and coconut milk and simmer for about 20 minutes. Add the tofu puffs and chicken and simmer for a further 10 minutes. Remove the chicken, shred finely and set aside.

Simmer the prawns in the soup for 3 minutes, or until just cooked, then remove and set aside. Taste the soup and adjust the seasoning as required.

LAKSA REMPAH (MAKES DOUBLE)

15 dried chillies, seeded and soaked in hot water for about 20 minutes

4 large red chillies, seeded

1 tablespoon belacan (shrimp paste)

6 shallots or 1 large brown onion, peeled and roughly chopped

10 garlic cloves, peeled

5 cm piece of fresh ginger, peeled and thickly sliced

5 cm piece of fresh galangal, peeled and thickly sliced

5 cm piece of fresh turmeric, peeled and thickly sliced

3 lemongrass stems, tender inner core only, roughly chopped

2 tablespoons ground coriander

6 candlenuts (or macadamia nuts)

CHILLI SAMBAL

5 dried chillies, soaked

3 large red chillies

2 eschalots or ½ small onion, roughly chopped

1 teaspoon belacan (shrimp paste)

½ cup (125 ml) peanut oil

a pinch of sugar

While the soup is cooking, prepare the remaining ingredients. Bring a large pot of water to the boil and cook the noodles according to the packet directions. While different brands will vary, generally hokkien noodles will just need to be blanched for a minute or so, while the vermicelli will need about 5 minutes. Boil the fish cake for about 2 minutes, or until puffed, then drain. Blanch the bean sprouts for 30 seconds. Boil the eggs for 7 minutes, then refresh in a basin of iced water and peel. Halve the eggs. Keep all the ingredients separate, so that you can build your laksa as you like it.

For the chilli sambal, blend all the chillies together with the eschalot and belacan. Heat a small saucepan over medium heat and fry the paste in the peanut oil for about 10 minutes, or until very fragrant, stirring frequently. Stir in the sugar and set aside for serving.

To assemble each laksa, warm a noodle bowl (by pouring in a bit of the hot soup, then returning the soup to the pot). Add some hokkien noodles, vermicelli, bean sprouts, egg, fish cake, prawn and chicken to the bowl. Ladle in some soup, then garnish with Vietnamese mint, cucumber and a big spoonful of chilli sambal. Serve immediately.

NOTE Vietnamese mint is known in Singapore and Malaysia as 'laksa leaf', and it is a natural accompaniment for laksa. The chilli sambal is necessary to really enhance the flavour of the dish, so don't skimp on it, even if you don't like too much heat. Laksa gets its name from the Hokkien or Cantonese for 'spicy sand' – a reference to the slightly gritty texture that comes from the addition of the ground dried shrimp.

This page: Katong laksa, otak-otak and a sugar cane juice, Katong
Opposite: Chicken & prawn laksa (page 234)

YIP CHOEI KHAU

THE CONNECTION BETWEEN FOOD AND CULTURE CAN BE SEEN
NO MORE CLEARLY THAN IN THE WAY SINGAPORE CELEBRATES ITS FOOD.

When you take away the rhythms of seasonality and harvest, it might seem like Singapore is just one continuous dinner party – 24/7, 365 days a year – but there is a lovely pace to eating around the year in Singapore, punctuated by events from the Chinese lunar calendar, such as New Year and the solstices, to feasts from Singapore's religious communities, such as Eid and Christmas.

Confucius in his teachings put a great deal of emphasis on the idea of feasting and marking important events through food. Feasting and celebration, Confucius advocated, was central to building a connection to community and family.

Yip Choei Khau has been making her Eight Treasure Duck for more than fifty years, and to watch her in full flight is a thing to behold. A small and delicate woman in her eighties, she whirls woks and hurls pots a person more than double her size would struggle with, all with the deft confidence of a true expert borne from year upon year of repetition.

Her duck is a traditional dish for Chinese New Year in Singapore, drawing from her Cantonese heritage and matching many of the traditional customs of the New Year.

It's a whole animal (often served with head and feet attached), which represents the togetherness and completeness of the family unit. It contains traditionally auspicious foods like Chinese sausage (cured meats are a relic from winter sacrifices of ancient times) and fat choy (a hair-like vegetable that is also a homophone for prosperity). Even the dish itself, with its eight treasures, symbolises great fortune.

A dish like this, developed over decades of celebration, joy and togetherness, is filled with more meaning and good fortune than even its eight treasures could ever symbolise.

This Cantonese dish, traditionally served on Chinese New Year's Eve, consists of a duck, fried and then steamed, stuffed with a collection of eight delicious ingredients, or 'treasures'. In Singapore, my friend Shem Leong's godmother, Yip Choei Khau, has been perfecting her version of the dish for more than fifty years.

EIGHT TREASURE DUCK

PREPARATION 40 MINUTES +
OVERNIGHT SOAKING
COOKING 3 HOURS
SERVES 6–8

¼ cup (60 ml) vegetable oil

3 kg whole duck, dried
   thoroughly

2–3 cups soaked fat choy
   (hair vegetable)

3 thin spring onions, sliced

STUFFING

10 garlic cloves, peeled

4 eschalots, sliced

1 cup (220 g) pearl barley

1 cup (160 g) dried chestnuts

1 cup dried lotus seeds

1 cup dried shiitake
   mushrooms

1 cup semi-cooked gingko
   nuts (vacuum-packed)

200 g lean pork shoulder,
   cut into 2 cm cubes

4 spring onions, finely
   chopped

4 Chinese sausages (lap
   cheong)

1 cup (160 g) water chestnuts

2 tablespoons light soy sauce

¼ teaspoon salt

1 teaspoon sugar

1 tablespoon oyster sauce

1 tablespoon sesame oil

1 tablespoon Chinese
   rice wine

Soak the pearl barley, dried chestnuts and lotus seeds separately in cold water overnight, then drain. Soak the dried shiitake mushrooms for 20 minutes; drain, then trim and discard the stems. Set aside.

For the duck, heat your wok over medium–high heat and add the oil. Fry the duck on all sides until the skin is golden. Reserving any oil left in the wok, place the duck in a deep, round roasting tin, big enough to fit the duck but small enough to fit inside a large pot or wok.

To make the stuffing, fry the whole garlic cloves and eschalots in the reserved oil in the wok over medium heat until golden, then remove and set aside in a bowl. Add the remaining stuffing ingredients to the wok in the order listed (adding the soaked ingredients together with the gingko nuts), and fry until fragrant, about 5 minutes in total.

Spoon the stuffing into a large bowl, trying to leave as much liquid in the wok as possible. Stuff the duck until tightly packed, capping off the end of the cavity with a few of the mushrooms, to stop the stuffing escaping. Any remaining stuffing can be tucked around the outer edges of the duck.

Spoon the remaining liquid in the wok over the duck, then cover very tightly with foil, completely sealing the duck.

To double-steam the duck, place a steaming trivet in the base of a pot or wok of water large enough to fit the entire duck dish inside. Alternatively, this is easily done in a steam oven.

Steam for 1 hour, then remove the foil. Sprinkle the fat choy over the top of the duck and spoon over the juices collected around the duck. Cover with the foil again and steam for further 1½ hours, topping up the water as needed, until the duck is very tender.

Serve garnished with the spring onion.

NOTE This is considered a lucky New Year's dish with the addition of fat choy, a green-black moss-like vegetable that looks a little like black hair and has a mild mushroomy flavour. 'Fat choy' sounds similar to a phrase meaning 'be prosperous'. You may have heard it in the traditional Cantonese New Year's greeting *gong hei fat choy*, which means 'Congratulations and be prosperous!'.

Originating in Klang, just outside Kuala Lumpur in Malaysia, bah kut teh is one of Singapore's most popular dishes. Literally meaning 'pork bone tea', it is defined by its rich, complex combination of medicinal herbs. Most people make theirs using pre-packaged spice packs, but I prefer to make my own soup base. They may look confusing, but these medicinal herbs are actually quite common ingredients in Chinese cooking. While most are available from a good Asian grocery, I buy mine from a Chinese herbalist. I've given their Mandarin pronunciations and Chinese character translations, so you can just show the herbalist your list.

BAH KUT TEH

PREPARATION 30 MINUTES
COOKING 2½ HOURS
SERVES 8

10 dried shiitake mushrooms

2 kg pork belly

1 kg pork ribs

3 whole garlic bulbs

3 tablespoons salt

2 tablespoons caster sugar

1 tablespoon white vinegar

½ cup (125 ml) soy sauce

6 cups (300 g) enoki mushrooms

sliced spring onion, to serve

coriander sprigs, to serve

HERB PACK

20 g Codonopsis pilosula (wén dǎng shēn) 纹党参

20 g Chinese angelica (dāng guī) 当归

10 g lovage root (chuān xiōng) 川芎

20 g Rehmannia glutinosa (shú dì) 熟地

5 slices licorice root (gān cǎo) 甘草

20 g Solomon's seal (yù zhú) 玉竹

2 pieces dried tangerine peel (chéng pí) 橙皮

15 g cassia bark (guì pí) 桂皮

3 star anise (bā jiǎo) 八角

1 teaspoon white peppercorns (bái hú jiāo) 白胡椒

Heat 16 cups (4 litres) water in a stockpot. Rinse the shiitake mushrooms and add them to the pot, then turn off the heat and let them soften for 20 minutes. Remove the mushrooms, then trim off the stalks using a pair of kitchen scissors. Return the caps to the pot, and place the pot back over the heat.

Wrap the ingredients for the herb pack in a double layer of muslin, and secure the pack with string. Add to the pot and simmer for 30 minutes.

While the herb pack is simmering, place the pork belly and ribs in a separate pot and cover with cold water. Bring the water to the boil and simmer for 20 minutes. Remove all the pork from the water and rinse to remove any scum.

Add the pork to the simmering soup base, along with the garlic bulbs, salt, sugar, vinegar and soy sauce. Simmer for about 1½ hours, until the pork is tender but not falling apart. Remove the pork from the soup and allow to cool slightly.

Add the enoki mushrooms to the soup and simmer for 5 minutes, or until the enoki are softened.

Cut the pork into small pieces, and separate the ribs. Divide the pork and ribs among serving bowls, then ladle the broth and mushrooms over. Scatter with spring onion and coriander sprigs.

Serve with cooked rice, youtiao (fried Chinese bread sticks) and sliced chillies in soy sauce on the side.

NOTE Bah kut teh is one of my favourite dishes in the world. It's great served with blanched iceberg lettuce, covered with oyster sauce and scattered with fried shallots. I love to eat the soup together with rice, adding pieces of fried youtiao for crunch and chilli for a bit of heat.

These Nyonya-style pineapple tarts are a favourite in Singapore. My Aunty Topsy makes the best tarts, and she's very kindly allowed me to share her recipe with you all. Seventy tarts might seem a lot to make in one batch, but please do make them all. They make a great gift. I should know, as I get a box from Aunty Topsy every time she comes to visit.

AUNTY TOPSY'S PINEAPPLE TARTS

PREPARATION 1½ HOURS +
30 MINUTES RESTING
COOKING 25 MINUTES FOR
THE JAM, AND 20–25 MINUTES
FOR EACH BATCH OF TARTS
MAKES ABOUT 70 TARTS

4½ cups (675 g) plain flour

2 cups (250 g) icing sugar
  mixture

2 cups (200 g) ground
  almonds

150 g cold butter

1 cup (250 g) lard

4 egg yolks, whites reserved
  for brushing

PINEAPPLE JAM

3 × 440 g tins crushed
  pineapple in syrup

1½ cups (330 g) sugar

1 teaspoon ground
  cinnamon

1 teaspoon ground cloves

For the pineapple jam, combine the pineapple, sugar, cinnamon and cloves in a saucepan over medium heat. Cook, stirring constantly, for about 20 minutes, or until the mixture turns golden brown, and the liquid has reduced. Allow to cool to room temperature, then chill in the fridge until ready to use.

For the pastry, combine the flour, icing sugar mixture, ground almonds, butter and lard in a food processor and pulse until the mixture resembles breadcrumbs. Add the egg yolks and 1 tablespoon cold water and pulse until a mass forms. Very lightly knead the dough in two batches, then wrap each batch in plastic wrap and refrigerate for 30 minutes.

Heat your oven to 180°C.

On a lightly floured board, roll a batch of pastry out to 1 cm thick. Cut out tart shapes, using a pineapple tart cutter or scalloped-edge cookie cutter. A pineapple tart cutter will make the indentation in the centre of the tart for the jam, but if you don't have one just make the indentation yourself with the back of a measuring tablespoon. Transfer the tart bases to a lined baking tray.

Fill each tart with a teaspoon of pineapple jam; you can roll the jam into a ball if you like.

Roll the leftover pastry into a thin sheet and cut into fine strips. Lay short strips of pastry on top of the jam, to create a cross or lattice pattern (Aunty Topsy makes a cross). Brush with the reserved egg whites.

Bake for 20–25 minutes, or until the pastry is lightly browned and cooked through. You can bake a few trays at once if you like.

Repeat with the remaining pastry and filling. You can store the tarts in an airtight container for up to 2 weeks.

NOTE It's hard to buy pineapple tart cutters outside Singapore, but you can use a cookie cutter instead. The tarts themselves are a popular souvenir to bring home from Singapore, but I think if you're going to bring someone tarts you may as well bring them a cutter too. You can buy the cutters in Singapore's Chinatown, and the tarts themselves just about everywhere.

Chef Lu Jiemin making Suzhou boat snacks, Suzhou, Jiangsu, China

INDEX

ACKNOWLEDGEMENTS

Destination Flavour would never have existed if it weren't for our Executive Producer Erik Dwyer, who took a small idea all around the world.

Special thanks also to:

Josh Martin, for continuing what we all started together.

Nicki Roller, who has steered this ship from the very beginning.

Simon Ryan, whose exceptional editing over the years has brought all these stories to life.

Scott Thomson, Mick de Montignie, Tim Thatcher, Rochelle Martin, Jason Franklin, Rachel Hardie and Olivia Hoopman, whose continuing guidance makes every show great.

Robin Probyn, Gilbert Farkas, Gary Lacroix and all the other camera operators, sound recordists and technical professionals who do such an amazing job on the road in near-impossible circumstances.

SBS, for their continuing faith in allowing us to tell both the exceptional stories and the ordinary ones.

The Australian Academy of Cinema and Television Arts for giving us a fancy award for all our hard work.

And the hundreds of other researchers, fixers, associate producers, composers, designers, editors, assistants, translators and other people who have made this series what it is.

I would also like to thank the team who have brought this book to life. Steve Brown for his ability to tell the story of food in a simple and subtle image, Berni Smithies for having the best eye in the business, Arum Shim for cooking the cuisines of the world without batting an eyelid, Jane Willson for her tireless work over the years to make this book happen, Loran McDougall and Katri Hilden for ensuring I make some sense, and all the rest of the talented team at Hardie Grant who take ideas from the air and make them a reality that we can hold in our hands and flip through page by page.

Thank you.

ABOUT THE AUTHOR

Instantly recognisable with his warm smile and topknot, award-winning *Destination Flavour* host and *MasterChef* winner Adam Liaw is one of Australia's favourite cooks, authors and television presenters. Articulate and witty, Adam brings a unique perspective to everything he does.

Born in Malaysia to an English-Singaporean mother and Hainanese Chinese father, Adam and his family lived in several countries throughout his youth, and his culinary influences are far-reaching. He was an active cook from an early age, regularly cooking for his parents and seven brothers and sisters from the time he was eight.

Adam holds university degrees in science and law, and practised law for eleven years, most recently as the Head of Legal and Business Affairs for Disney Interactive, Asia Pacific based in Tokyo. His love affair with food and cooking blossomed during this time and he returned to Australia in 2009 to compete in *MasterChef*. In July 2010 over five million people tuned in to watch him win the show's second series. His victory remains the most watched non-sporting event in Australian television history.

In 2012 he began filming *Destination Flavour* with SBS, with *Destination Flavour Scandinavia* taking out the ACTAA award for Best Lifestyle Program in 2016.

Adam is also a regular columnist for *Sunday Life*, *The Sydney Morning Herald*, *The Courier Mail*, *The Age*, *The Guardian*, *The Wall Street Journal* and *SBS online*, as well as the author of five best-selling cookbooks: *Two Asian Kitchens*, *Asian After Work*, *Adam's Big Pot*, *Asian Cookery School* and *The Zen Kitchen*.

He is Unicef Australia's National Ambassador for Nutrition and was named the Goodwill Ambassador for Japanese Cuisine in ackowledgement of his significant contributions to promoting regional Japanese cuisine in Australia.

Adam lives in Sydney with his wife, Asami, their son, Christopher, and daughter, Anna. He speaks English, Japanese and basic Mandarin. Between his TV commitments and writing cookbooks, recipes and columns, he makes regular appearances at events and food festivals, and he usually has time to post a tweet or two.

Pages 252–3:
Naha, Okinawa, Japan
Opposite: The ancient town
of Hongcun, Anhui, China

This book uses 20 ml (¾ fl oz) tablespoons; cooks with 15 ml (½ fl oz) tablespoons should be generous with their tablespoon measurements.

Metric cup measurements are used, i.e. 250 ml (8½ fl oz) for 1 cup; in the US a cup is 237 ml (8 fl oz), so American cooks should be generous with their cup measurements; in the UK, a cup is 284 ml (9½ fl oz), so British cooks should be scant with their cup measurements.

Published in 2018 by Hardie Grant Books, an imprint of Hardie Grant Publishing

Hardie Grant Books (Melbourne)
Building 1, 658 Church Street
Richmond, Victoria 3121

Hardie Grant Books (London)
5th & 6th Floors
52–54 Southwark Street
London SE1 1UN

hardiegrantbooks.com

All rights reserved. No part of this publication may be reproduced, stored in a retrieval system or transmitted in any form by any means, electronic, mechanical, photocopying, recording or otherwise, without the prior written permission of the publishers and copyright holders.

The moral rights of the author have been asserted.

Copyright text © Adam Liaw 2018
Copyright photography © Steve Brown (6 (bottom right), 17, 19, 27, 31, 35, 37, 38, 48, 51, 54, 61, 70, 73, 77, 79, 82, 85, 87, 90, 93, 94, 105, 106, 119, 122, 125, 126, 129, 131, 133, 134, 138–9, 141, 147, 150, 155, 157, 159, 160, 165, 166, 169, 171, 176, 178, 181, 183, 186, 197, 198, 203, 211, 213, 214, 221, 226, 228, 231, 233, 236, 242, 245); SBS (all other photos) 2018
Copyright design © Hardie Grant Publishing 2018

 A catalogue record for this book is available from the National Library of Australia

NATIONAL LIBRARY OF AUSTRALIA

Destination Flavour
ISBN 978 1 74379 448 7

10 9 8 7 6 5 4 3 2 1

Publishing Director: Jane Willson
Managing Editor: Marg Bowman
Project Editor: Loran McDougall
Editor: Katri Hilden
Design Manager: Jessica Lowe
Designer: Michelle Mackintosh
Typesetter: Megan Ellis
Food Photographer: Steve Brown
Stylist: Bernadette Smithies
Home Economist: Arum Shim
Production Manager: Todd Rechner
Production Coordinator: Tessa Spring

Colour reproduction by Splitting Image Colour Studio

Printed in China by 1010 Printing International Limited